P9-ARH-601

ANCESTORS

A PROJECT OF THE *BOSTON REVIEW* ARTS IN SOCIETY PROGRAM

This publication was made possible by generous support from
THE WILLIAM AND FLORA HEWLETT FOUNDATION

Editors-in-Chief Deborah Chasman & Joshua Cohen

Managing Editor and Arts Editor Adam McGee

Senior Editor Matt Lord

Engagement Editor Rosie Gillies

Manuscript and Production Editor Hannah Liberman

Contributing Editors Adom Getachew, Walter Johnson, Amy Kapczynski, Robin D.G. Kelley, Lenore Palladino

Contributing Arts Editor Ed Pavlić

2020 Annual Poetry Contest Judge Alexis Pauline Gumbs

2020 Aura Estrada Short Story Contest Judge Ivelisse Rodriguez

Editorial Assistants Tadhg Larabee, Meghana Mysore, Katya Schwenk, & Jason Vanger

Marketing and Development Manager Dan Manchon

Special Projects Manager María Clara Cobo

Finance Manager Anthony DeMusis III

Printer Sheridan PA

Board of Advisors Derek Schrier (chair), Archon Fung, Deborah Fung, Alexandra Robert Gordon, Richard M. Locke, Jeff Mayersohn, Jennifer Moses, Scott Nielsen, Robert Pollin, Rob Reich, Hiram Samel, Kim Malone Scott

Interior Graphic Design Zak Jensen & Alex Camlin

Cover Design Alex Camlin

Ancestors is *Boston Review* Forum 17 (46.1)

To become a member, visit bostonreview.net/membership/

For questions about donations and major gifts, contact Dan Manchon, dan@bostonreview.net

For questions about memberships, call 877-406-2443 or email Customer_Service@bostonreview.info.

Boston Review
PO Box 390568
Cambridge, MA 02139-0568

ISSN: 0734-2306 / ISBN: 978-1-946511-55-3

CONTENTS

RUPTURES & TRANSFORMATIONS

ONWARD

EDITORS' NOTE

Alexis Pauline Gumbs, Adam McGee,
Ed Pavlić, & Ivelisse Rodriguez

ANCESTORS OPENS AND CLOSES with stories by authors who are now ancestors and each, in its own way, blasts the reader into the heavens. We could think of no better place to start than with a story that describes the birth of an ancestor: in Binyavanga Wainaina's (1971–2019) recently rediscovered "Binguni!," we are led through a psychedelic fantasia of the African afterlife which reassures that death is only a beginning. And then Izumi Suzuki's (1949–1986) newly translated "Night Picnic" concludes *Ancestors* in a distant future in which the characters ask—and are at a loss to answer—the question: *What does it mean to be human?*

When we first began imagining *Ancestors*, the second annual Arts in Society anthology, Toni Morrison had recently died and we'd been rereading her essay "Rootedness: The Ancestor as Foundation" (1984). In it, she suggests that a defining characteristic of African American literature is what she calls "the presence of an ancestor." And for Morrison, the ancestral presence leads directly to "the community . . . an implied 'we' . . . which is to say, yes, the work must be political."

We were so struck by this formulation—and its intrinsic challenge—that we wanted to see what would happen if we asked some of the most talented writers we know (including our contest entrants): *What does it look like if you summon the presence of the ancestors into your art?*

The result is what you hold in your hands. The answers we received were diverse and exciting beyond our wildest imaginings, but we feel certain that readers will take from the book an enriched sense of what it means to be a human living in a time, among other times, and to be part of a lineage, among other lineages, to have questions inherited from the past—as well as other "beyonds"—that shape our lives and will, no doubt, continue to shape the future on which we leave our impress.

The book is divided into three sections, "Origins," "Ruptures & Transformations," and "Onward," which reflect our sense of how these pieces speak to our deepest beginnings, to how the tragedies of the past shape us, and to how we carry the mantle of the ancestors forward.

When we started this project, we could never have imagined that it would conclude in the midst of a world-historic pandemic that has left millions dead and millions more gutted by loss. It sometimes feels it's impossible to think of anything else—like Prospero's famous utterance, "Every third thought shall be my grave."

But we hope that this book will serve as a summoning spell for readers, invoking ancestral wisdom—which for Morrison meant engaged awareness of each other—to guide us all into and through whatever comes next.

ORIGINS

BINGUNI!

Binyavanga Wainaina, introduced by Achal Prabhala

KENYAN WRITER Binyavanga Wainaina (1971–2019) was among the greatest of his generation. A winner of the Caine Prize for African Writing, in the final decade of his life he had become as well a celebrated speaker, and was even named to *TIME*'s list of "Most Influential People in the World."

Knowing him was not unlike reading him: he could be dazzling, compelling, and exhausting all at once. The unusual velocity of his most famous essays, especially "How to Write About Africa" (2005) and "I Am a Homosexual, Mum" (2014), means that many readers think of his writing as characterized by polemic and raw confession. But his work could also be gentle, loving, and playful, and nowhere are these qualities more evident than in his fiction.

"Binguni!" (1996) was Binyavanga's first published work of fiction. In 2017, after battling multiple strokes and a range of physical problems that left him dispirited, Binyavanga wrote to me to ask for help in recovering it.

It was set in a heaven that African Ancestors went to die. I am desperate to find it. I remember the lead character was called Jango. There was a sentence in it about his mind being like a "helium balloon." It was published on a website . . . called purification.com. Is there no way of recovering it?

After a futile week of searching through a range of water purification projects on the African continent, thanks to his hazy memory and his lifelong disregard for spelling things accurately, I almost gave up. Then I turned to the shining jewel that is the Internet Archive, and miraculously stumbled upon purefiction.com, which I quickly realized had been a vibrant hub for new writing in the early 1990s.

Reading "Binguni!" in 2017 was magical for Binyavanga—and for me. To anyone who followed his coming out in 2014, Binyavanga's broadsides against the Pentecostal church are well known. Less known is that, toward the end of his life, he became deeply interested in African precolonial spirituality. His coming out had been followed by a series of devastating health setbacks. Perhaps this spiritual quest fit into a larger quest—a liberation from the past and a connection to a new future.

But it was also surprising. Binyavanga was, for most of his life, the least spiritual person I knew. To rediscover "Binguni!" with him was a revelation, then: not merely for the beauty of the prose, but for what it taught me about its author. Every single thing he spent his last years on Earth being consumed by—spirituality, sexuality, discovery, and death—is in this story, his very first.

Binyavanga was notoriously careless about his archive. And yet it puzzled me that he would have let something as fresh and wonderful as this stay hidden for so long. Now I realize it might have been deliberate. A lone strategy for survival in a life marked by the absence of any. Perhaps he thought better of revealing so much about his interior self until he was absolutely ready—until his own helium-ballooned mind made its final ascent, knocking at the edge of the stratosphere with nowhere left to go.

—Achal Prabhala

Two goldfish were arguing in their bowl, "If there is no God, who changes our water every week?"

Allotropy (ə-'lä-trə-pē) n. the property of certain elements to exist in two or more distinct forms

I

Dawn, December 27, 1999

Jango had often pictured his imagination as a helium-filled balloon, rather than one containing air. As he rose above the wreckage of the car, a whole-body feeling came over him. His life had ended, the string was cut, and his imagination was free to merge with reality. He felt immensely liberated—like he was flexing muscles that had not been used in a long time.

Oh, to stretch! His body felt loose-limbed and weightless and his mind poised to soar. How could he have stayed in cramped earthliness for so long? How could he have forgotten this feeling? Had he not once danced with stars and had dalliances with gods?

Was he dreaming? Or was this part of some spectral past life? He felt no trauma of the type normally associated with violent death. Right now, he was rather piqued that he had missed out on the nonstop partying that was taking place all over the world. He hugged himself and found that his body seemed intact. He found it odd that he did not seem to feel the trepidation he would have expected if there was a possibility that he was destined for Pastor Vimba's "LAKE OF FIYYRRE!" that starred a leering Red Devil and promised "EEETERNALL DAMNATIONNN!" He giggled at the thought. "Tsk, tsk, Jango," he said to himself. "You're getting above yourself!"

Oddly enough, right now the thought of going to "Heaven" and spending eternity dressed in white robes, blissfully ensconced behind Pearly Gates while drinking nectar or listening to harps was depressing. After spending most of his life in Johannesburg, and especially after the hedonism of the past few days, the "fires of hell" acquired a certain appeal.

There was another possible destination though. His father's mania. To become an esteemed ancestor, as Zulu tradition dictated. Yet he could not visualize himself tolerating eternity as an "Outraged Ancestor," imposing droughts and plagues on disobedient descendants and anybody else who happened to be in the vicinity. Ancestor worship was a religion his father had tried to drum (quite often literally) into his head, and it was one he had discarded with relief. The concept of ancestors scrutinizing and guiding peoples' lives had always inspired images of power-mad old voyeurs playing African roulette (giggle, giggle . . . whom shall we play with next—Rwanda?)

What if one descended from a long line of arseholes?

He thought to himself that if he had a choice, he would not mind being dispatched to some sort of Spectral Cyberspace, if such a fanciful place could exist. Hmm, yes. Maybe he was on his way to a place where nobody would dictate to him how to live his life.

Oops.

Afterlife.

Pah! Banish the thought. There were probably harp-playing Censors lovingly denying souls/spirits/whatever their daily fix of Ambrosia if they did not conform.

As he floated with a sort of predetermined aimlessness, he delighted in his new rubber-bandy self, vaguely wondering why he seemed to have carried his body with him. Surely his real body was still getting intimate with the mangled metal of his car?

He looked down at the surrealistic African visage below him. It was as if, as the Earth relinquished its pull on him, he relinquished all the trauma that he expected to have felt after the accident; relinquished all the weighty emotions and burdensome responsibilities that did not endear themselves to his new weightless self.

Or maybe he was still stoned from the party.

Around and below him, the Earth had decided to stake its claim. A sudden gust of wind whipped itself up into a frenzy of anger and lightning seared the ground. Thunder roared as if backing up the sky's claim on him. Massive, engorged clouds lay low, and gave birth to reluctant raindrops.

This drama had no physical effect on him. It seemed that he was in a dimension beyond Earth now. He could not remain unmoved by her mourning though. As the wind wailed in fury, he mimicked it, roaring his farewell to her.

Meanwhile, fast asleep at her home in Diepkloof, Soweto, Mama Jango moaned as the cloud of unformed premonition that floated past her house darkened her pedestrian dreams. A shadow of loss chilled her briefly. Later she would wonder, and trusty Pastor Vimba would come up with a satisfactory supernatural explanation.

Meanwhile, exultation welled in Jango as he looked below him and saw the grand panorama of the storm-enlivened city below him. A powerful love for what had been his adopted home for twenty-seven years overwhelmed him. Wordsworth's famous sonnet, a personal favorite, came to mind and he laughed, stretching his arms wide and bellowing in exultation:

> Earth has not anything to show more fair:
> Dull would he be of soul who could pass by
> A sight so FUCKING touching in its majesty:
> This City now doth, like a garment, wear . . .

Suddenly a force lifted the flat veldt and highways below him as if they were merely a tablecloth and swallowed them. In no time everything earthly below him—the mine dumps, squatter camps, towers, domes, theaters, and temples of Johannesburg—disappeared the same way. Evaporated by something that seemed to have no substance or form.

Jango found himself surrounded by nothingness.

And all that mighty heart is lying still.

Wainaina

· · ·

Stasis.

Silence so absolute, it screamed louder than anything he had ever experienced.

The sensation was terrifying. Utter nothingness surrounded him. There was no light, no darkness, nothing to feel or touch. Unearthly cold imprisoned his body. He began to shake and shudder, but soon even his shudders became sluggish and eventually ceased. He was immobile.

In the absolute silence, he could not tell whether he was still floating. An excruciating numbness began to spread all over his body. Soon his body lost all feeling. He lowered his eyes to see what was happening, and to his horror saw that something was eliminating it with a devastating silence.

As if it had never been there.

Finally, only the feeling that his mind was present remained, and it screamed into the nothingness to make itself heard. It tried all manner of activities to convince itself that it would be all right, but waves and waves of self-doubt assaulted it as it found nothing to compare or process. Nothing to perceive.

Not even an echo.

Shutdown began in some areas of his mind, and the rest reacted by exaggerating their most recent functions. Oh shit! This is it! He thought frantically to himself, This is how it ends. Huge, terribly distorted images thrust themselves to the forefront of his consciousness as it tried to resist the terrible finality of its surroundings. Now all that remained were the screams of tortured metal, flashing lights, his crazed screams, and the smell of feces and smoke. His mind accepted these gratefully as evidence that there was existence, that he did exist. These scenes played themselves over and over as the shutdown continued undeterred, becoming more and more scrambled and indecipherable as more functions shut down.

Then there was just nothing.

II

"Is it a kind of dream . . . following the river of death downstream?"
—Art Garfunkel

Something enveloped him luxuriously. Light, or a beginning of awareness?

Starting with his toes he tingled with it and it spread until every part of him glowed with its warmth. It was the strangest feeling, as if he had been recreated as light; his shape a memory of his earthly body. Nothingness still surrounded him, but he was now a spiritual glowworm, cocooned in what he could only think of as a life-fire. Every part of him took flame, as his body memory emphatically affirmed and embraced his being. Tiny raptures exploded all over his mind; life thrills and memories concentrated into tiny capsules of pure feeling.

Again, his recent trauma seemed to have had no major effect on him. He did not want to try to understand it. He felt so good.

Children dressed in all manner of cultural pajamas floated past him, playing in their dreamscapes as if this place was home. Again, that feeling of acquaintance with this place struck him. This time he was sure that, at some early part of his life, he had straddled this place and Earth without conflict. Oh, to bathe in this light again!

He felt a fleeting sadness that these children would be soon tethered to life on Earth as its chains embraced them with ever-increasing possessiveness. Don't wake me up, mummy!

"Enjoy it while you can, kids," he thought.

He looked above him and saw his naked body mirrored and magnified in a huge translucent gelatinous mass that covered the sky. Saw the long black limbs, the chunky muscle. The hated feet were stretched taut. Saw the face, a rictus of anticipation. Then his eyes trampolined the soft large lips and clambered up the jutting mountains that were his cheekbones, scratching themselves against his toothbrush stubble on their way up.

Looking down from the summit, two large eye-pools below hypnotized them. Irresistibly drawn to their twins, they dived off the cliff into themselves and his soul swallowed them.

Light! Oozing out of the mirrored eyes. Light stained brown with their color lit the cloud, dazzling Jango with its brilliance. Oh, the ecstasy! It was his light! His essence! He could feel it coming alive in his body, burning its way up from his feet to neck, roller-coastering through the pathways of his mind, setting them alight with its force, then blazing out of his eyes to meet its reflection. They made contact and the universe around him exploded.

He was somewhere else.

. . .

His eyes took time to adjust to the light. He was in a world that seemed comprised of nothing but living color. Dancing light was all around him. Heavenly shadows? Directly in front of him, a small tornado of light twisted itself and took on the shape of a person. Then it began to fade and assumed more human features.

An old man had materialized before him. An extremely sour-faced old man. His hair was waist long and in dreadlocks. He wore a three-piece suit, complete with bowler hat. Instead of a tie, there was what looked like a desiccated human ear at the end of a leather thong around his neck. The old man was squatting, African-fashion, and hovered three feet in the air fiddling with the ear as though it was some kind of talisman.

It was around this time that it occurred to Jango that this was no Heavenly Emissary. His helium balloon began to lose altitude.

Bleak, bitter eyes turned to face him.

"Ah, you're the newcomer," he began. "I presume my accent is comprehensible to you. I learned it in anticipation of your arrival. Let me see. . . . Black, English-speaking, Dekaff, I believe you would call it . . . er . . . with a slight urban Zulu accent . . . car accident on the Johannesburg-Pretoria highway. Pity about the BMW. . . ."

Jango did not find this dour-peeping Thabo amusing. Was that really a human ear? A white man's ear? Did they not have a Public Relations department here? This man was more bitter than malaria medication. Yup, no chance this was Heaven. Oh shit! This was either Hell or Rwandan Rouletteville.

Wainaina

"Hima Tata!" he burst out. "Where is this place and who the—er—heaven are you? Is this some sort of celestial prank?"

Malaria Face adopted an even sourer expression—if that were possible. "I have often thought so. I am Kariuki, and you are now in what we call African Binguni, part of the Otherworld. Souls here have complete freedom to explore just how mad they can be. You would not believe what perversions prowl in this place. I left Binguni in disgust. Nothing is sacred to these immoral Immortals. I am waiting to be transferred to African Presbyteria, you'll do well to do the same. Their harp band is famous all over the heavens!"

Jango shuddered. Any place this anally overburdened body-part collector did not like was probably his kind of Heaven. This African Binguni place sounded like fun.

A thin smile distorted the old man's features. "I understand you are one of the highlights at the Millennial Celebrations, they have chosen you for their insane new experiment. I do not envy you. Now enough chitchat, I will summon Mshale on the Supernet, and he will take you to the millennial festivities."

"Wait a second, who is Mshale and what experiment?"

The Churl harrumphed: "He is one of your ancestors, a disreputable pervert even by the standards here. Now shut up, they will explain all to you. My work in this hellhole is finished."

One of the floating cloud-like things turned into a large screen. With considerable surprise, Jango recognized what looked like a poached version of the Netscape Navigator on the screen. The only real difference was that "Binguniscape" was what was written in the left-hand corner. Jango dazedly wondered what they did about copyright as he watched Kariuki reach out a hand and scribble on the screen: HTTP://AFTERLIFE

And a website appeared on the screen:

WELCOME TO THE HEAVENLY WEB! THIS MESSAGE IS SPONSORED BY THE SUPPLIERS OF COMPUTER SOUL-STUFF TO BINGUNI

Kariuki mumbled, "Can't be bothered to learn drumsong compuspeak," and wrote "AA.JangotoMshale@AncestralFair" on the screen. Jango was unable to express his astonishment as he suddenly found himself surrounded by darkness.

First to appear was a blue light that slowly formed itself into a banner reading: "WELCOME TO THE MILLENNIAL ANCESTRAL FAIR"

Then the ground began to unravel itself: an unrolling carpet of hard, unrelenting African earth, briefly tinted blue by the now fading light of the banner. Grassland, acacia trees, and scrub covered the ground. In the distance, Jango could see feeding herds of wildebeest and zebra. A minuscule shaft of light appeared on the horizon, growing rapidly and becoming the sun. Its bright white light drowned the banner, then it turned red and sunset burned the ground and trees with its color. On the horizon, the light shadows danced, numinous mirages of humanity. From a distance Jango heard drums beating, and they grew louder—seeming to be coming from closer and closer. He stood still in fascination as this supernatural Cyberdrama unfolded.

Wainaina

As he dazedly wondered who designed this Supernatural Website, an enormous bellow interrupted the download and it was followed by a string of curses in a combination of Zulu, English, and languages Jango didn't even know existed. Somewhere in the background he could hear music.

"HAYIBO! THAT FUCKING KARIUKI'S DONE IT TO ME AGAIN!"

The voice sounded much closer now and a body had begun to materialize next to Jango. The huge sweating figure that appeared in front of him could only have been the Notorious Mshale, his great-grandfather. Dressed like a cross between Elvis and a Hollywood version of "What an African Warrior Should Look Like," he wore a leopard-skin loincloth that had ridden up his thigh, leaving the head of a huge dangling penis clearly visible below the hem. A leather waistcoat studded with rhinestones barely covered his heavily muscled torso. His hair was dreadlocked, pomaded, and piled on his head—sort of an Elvis-becomes-a-Rastafari hairdo.

The man even wore blue suede shoes.

Mumbling to himself in Zulu, he tugged the hem of the loincloth down and rearranged his organ. "Damned Internet!" he boomed. "It really does pick its moments. One day soon I'll get revenge on that prig of a Gatekeeper!"

"Hello, Tat'omkulu, I am Jango."

Mshale laughed. "Do I look like a grandfather to you! Call me Mshale. I don't stand on ceremony. Sorry about my outfit—I was performing a striptease for some maidens from Arabian Binguni. I understand that you're another one who doesn't speak Zulu, eh?

You don't know what you're missing, bhuti, it is the sexiest language in Binguni. Yo! You should hear me doing Elvis in Zulu, the man himself has come to Binguni to see me perform!"

Jango, the free-thinking, "anything goes" liberal was beginning to feel a tad conservative and old-fashioned. What would his "the Ancestors are governing your morals" father have to say about this rock-and-roll-in-the-hay ancestor?

"How did you die by the way?"

"I had attended a druggy New Age bash, one of those 'I love the whole world' millennial parties, and on the way home my car somewhat overeagerly decided to hug a lamppost—at a hundred and fifty kilometers an hour. . . ."

"And the rest is Ancestral, eh! Hayibo! You're lucky to have such a glamorous death! Would you believe the blasted flu killed me! Me! The great Induna, lover of all women! Come on, we don't have much time. I have a roomful of maidens baying for my presence. Let's get to the party!"

Jango's hand was grabbed by a huge, horny paw. Mshale mumbled something in Zulu and their surroundings disappeared.

Before any scenes appeared before Jango, the smell assaulted him, pungent and tropical, the smell of a marketplace or a marriage feast. Frenzy, sweat, musk, and sensual heat—the smell of abandon.

The noise followed. It was loud and disorganized. He could hear laughter, conversation, and song, in a bewildering assortment of languages. It did not sound like anything Jango had ever encountered. It was as if he could hear every individual's input and everybody's drone all at once. The sheer intensity of it was unnerving and his mind struggled to unscramble the confusion. Soon, amid the gibberish, he could hear snatches of sounds that his consciousness could make sense of.

"SALE! SALE! ENHANCE YOUR GLOW, SURF MY NEW SOULSITE FOR THE BARGAIN PRICE OF ONLY TWO HUMANITIES OF PAIN!"

"SPECTRAL SEX . . . CHECK OUT WHAT MY GENE-MEMORY HAS COME UP WITH!"

Even a jingle?

"SOUL-SYTE DESIGNS . . . FOR A TRULY SPIRITUAL SITE—SOOUUL SYTE!!"

"SIGN UP FOR A COURSE IN THE NIGGAHS NEW DRUMSONG COMPUSPEAK . . . KEYBOARDS ARE PASSÉ!"

"MAMA SQUEEZA'S SOUL BREW . . . AN UNEARTH-LY HIGH!"

Going off to the soul clinic, I haven't been feeling ecstatic lately.

"THE 'PHECAL MATYRS' IN CONCERT! TAKE A TRIP ON THE DARK SIDE!"

"PUTTY & THE BLOWFISH: BODY MEMORY REPAIRS"

"JOIN THE CYBER-BER QUICKENING! ACHIEVE NIRVANA!"

"EXPERIENCE PURE AGONY . . . RECENT ARRIVALS FROM RWANDA!"

"TIRED OF JOY? TAKE PACKAGE TOUR TO BINGUNI DARK. ECSTATIC AGONY!"

"DUMP SOME PAIN ON A DICTATOR HERE"

Before he had time to get his bearings, they were plunged into a maelstrom of humanity. What seemed to be a crossroad of souls, rushing in all directions, each hindering the other. Faces thrust themselves in his sight as he dumbly followed Mshale. Huge grins as if from convex and concave mirrors surrounded him, laughing, chanting, singing, arguing.

They were illuminated by revelation, faces overcome with amazement, eyes shining with enthusiasm, pupils dilated with joy, love, passion, and intensity. There seemed to be no logic to their appearance. Bodies danced with scant regard for anatomy or physics. A few passed right through him, leaving varied and intimate flavors of themselves in him. With every step, a swarm of locusts went wild in his insides.

The people who passed through his body seemed to infect it with their exuberance, and he found it hard to contain himself. A flood of hysterical laughter rose, threatening to engulf his control. He clenched his teeth and swallowed it down. It was promptly replaced by nausea. He much preferred that.

"Are you all right, bhuti?" Jango nodded. "Keep yourself together, we're nearly there. The Welcome is usually more restrained, but we're celebrating, and we have been waiting long for you."

Finally, with Jango feeling rather like he had overdosed on something illegal, they arrived at the Millennial Fair, or maybe it had found them. Jango was not sure what was where, or if anything was anywhere. "This is a dream," he thought. "I have smoked too much pot and I am tripping."

He did not need to pinch himself for Mshale's sledgehammer of a hand walloped his back and brought him to a stinging awareness of his surroundings.

"Welcome!" boomed Mshale. "What do you think of this madhouse, eh?"

· · ·

What a madhouse it was. Unearthly chaos. And its sensory impact was devastating. He felt as if the world he was in was in constant motion, there was no foundation. His senses were being overwhelmed from every direction.

There was no time to absorb or digest the impact, and even if there had been he did not think that he would have made any logic of what was going on around him. It was as if people here expressed themselves with all senses through a multitude of media and dimensions. He could feel communication bypass his conscious mind and flow into his subconscious. Buttons rusty with disuse were pushed and doors opened to raw, virgin sections of his mind.

What was most terrifying was that, for the first time he could recall, the thin crust that was logic, civilization, reason, and manners was not in control, it had gone off to a far place and was helplessly observing the body it had served so loyally for twenty-seven years being taken over by pure primal sensation.

He laughed wildly, thinking, "Shit, now this is Multimedia!" The laugh turned into a growl, then exploded into an animal screech. His mind was wide open with all the filters gone, and its unprotected core was being singed by uncontrolled input.

From far away he heard Mshale's voice saying harshly, "Sorry, bhuti, hold on for a bit and I will seal you off from this." Amid the pandemonium that surrounded him, he glimpsed a flash of dreadlocks and he felt Mshale's huge arms around his body. Then something that felt like cool water entered his overheated consciousness and covered it. Relief! His mind attempted a brief resistance against this foreign invader, but a deep gravelly voice crooned it to acquiescence. Finally, he felt himself completely surrounded by a pungent maleness. There was an almost sexual intimacy in the feeling that was disturbing. All his five senses could perceive Mshale completely. Coarse facial hair thrusting through skin and a shock of testosterone.

He remained quiescent as his mind calmed down. Mshale's grip on it was solid and nothing penetrated. After a while, Mshale's grip relaxed, and his consciousness began to communicate softly with Jango's.

"This is my fault, bhuti, we were so excited by your arrival, we forgot that you have not been formatted to face us all together."

He chuckled, and Jango shuddered at the soothing vibration of it.

"You should feel complimented, it is not so often I soul-merge with a man."

He could feel that the sinews of Mshale's body intertwined with his as they gripped his body powerfully, calming the violent shudders. He could hear vibrations and it seemed that somebody was communicating with Mshale, a deeper, more resonant sentience, not as gravelly or harsh.

"Jango," throbbed Mshale. "I have spoken to Senkou. He is an old soul, the one who chose you for this mission. He will replace me as your mind's environment, he's better at this than I am."

That elicited a brief flutter of panic. "Relax," a murmur throbbed. "It will be seamless."

He could feel Mshale's essence seep out of him as another replaced him. Initially, it was difficult to discern the flavor of this person as it mingled with Mshale's pungency. Gradually, he had the sense of a deep, almost bottomless personality: it resonated antiquity and calmness. In contrast to Mshale, he could feel little of this person's physical presence. Another difference was the bizarre sensation that certain essences of himself occurred in this person. This part of the foreign consciousness instantly entered Jango's consciousness and merged with its twin, giving him a feeling of peculiar comfort.

"I wish you peace and many raptures."

What a voice. Ripples as a pebble sank in deep waters.

DNA AND OUR TWENTY-FIRST-CENTURY ANCESTORS

Duana Fullwiley

SOME OF MY ANCESTORS might live just up the street. They are the people who own the black camper van with a decal brandishing the words "Irish Pride." I pass their house on my walks, a little unsure where ethnic importance might blur into white nationalism even in the hills of Oakland, California. The sticker, a simple bloc design in green and white, joins the two potentially menacing terms in a crossword. The middle *I* hinges them in a calm, clover-colored Celtic cross that sends my brain thinking of meadows to flee the idea of possible racial hatred. Lightly freckled, with age-bleached red hair like my mother, the man recently waved to me from one of several cars parked on their auto-filled lot, where the couple has taken to hanging out on sunny afternoons during COVID-19.

One tribe down. Hundreds, possibly thousands, more to go.

The next most obvious might be the Yoruba, somewhere among the people on my dad's side. One, who arrived from Lagos a few years ago, is a friend who lives down the hill in the flats. They refuse to choose a gender and are onto bigger issues, like devising an AI to catalog and then create 3D replicas of all of the stolen African artifacts in the British Museum.

What if my middle-aged, self-affirming Irish American neighbors had lived in Salt Lake City as children, with parents who were willing to be sampled for a 1980s French study that went on to furnish "European" DNA to scientists around the world? What if my Nigerian friend, whose father is a transnational scientist, was one of the Yoruba chosen for the International Haplotype Map project that took genetic material for a global database from family trios (mother, father, and one child) beginning in 2002?

These contemporary humans could very well have been counted among the human reference samples that have now become entrenched as genetically "ancestral" for people who purchase DNA tests such as those offered by companies like Ancestry and 23andMe. Sales of these direct-to-consumer kits now make up a multibillion-dollar industry that has tested millions of people, giving them ancestry results like "63 percent Irish and 47 percent Yoruba." In reality, the world will never know who in particular was initially sampled for most reference datasets. The names and personal information are confidential. Little more than donors' geographical location or some aspect of an ethnic, racial, or national moniker are publicized. The point is, there is nothing inherent in who my prideful neighbors or my smart friend are as people that would exclude their DNA from the stores of biological raw material used to manufacture the modern-day product called genetic ancestry.

As such, those who have given their DNA are people, like my friend and the Irish up the street, who are intricately bound up with complex identities, passions, and existences like the rest of us. They too, in Whitman's words, *contain multitudes*—that cannot be reduced to genetic sequences fixed in antiquated time. Their sequences of course contain allelic variation, along with even more similarities, when compared across the board. These too are reduced to select markers that have been culled to statistically differentiate people by geographic location (more on that later). In this process, DNA itself becomes amplified, literally and figuratively. Its new existence—phenomenally both larger and smaller than life itself—shuttles between the spaces of laboratories and everyday people's lives via the tableaux of apps on computer and smart phone screens. "Ancestry paintings," as one company calls the display of its autosomal DNA test results, take different forms. A common feature is that they attempt to convey the onlooker's intimate belonging to the world's people through colorful maps, with clear arrows indicating relation to distant lands, alongside lists of scribed identities that combine to signify the past—spatially and temporally.

Outside of labs, however, the ancestors continue on with their diverse, unpredictable, and very twenty-first-century preoccupied lives all around us.

AS AN ANTHROPOLOGIST, I have spent the past two decades studying how geneticists' beliefs and cultural ideas shape how they draw up the scientific world, both for themselves and for larger publics. One of the immediately striking aspects of autosomal genetic ancestry tests among everyday people is the emphasis on, well, ancestors.

This is not surprising since geneticists themselves use the term "ancestral" to refer to the people from whom they collect DNA to serve as reference samples. Scientists even sometimes swap the word ancestral with "parental," a more intimate yet more obviously personified term within a parlance of present-day family. Talking about these samples as assumed ancestors, or parents, originated as a way to frame services for potential American consumers, patients, study subjects, and curious genealogy mappers.

When I've given public talks, exchanged ideas with audiences at museums, lectured at universities, and conversed with friends and family about their genetic ancestry results, one thing is clear. People most often think that the DNA tests they buy are telling them something about long ago human DNA, bits of themselves directly shared with humans from another time. There is a look of disbelief, and a lot of questions that follow, when I tell them that most often their DNA is being compared to plain old humans in the here and now. With the rare exception of some Neanderthal DNA sequence variants that 23andMe uses for a specific product called the Neanderthal Ancestry Report, the DNA used in ancestry kits is not sequenced from old bones. It is not from ancient ancestors who lived on the Earth long ago. Rather, it is extracted from fellow contemporary *Homo sapiens*.

I call these unknown assumed ancestors the *Today People* to cut through the many layers of confusion that ancestry testing has created for consumers to sift through. The Today People are individuals who (withstanding the possibility of recent death) are currently busily alive in the same ways we are. They too have given their DNA to scientists. Yet most did so without being asked to pay. Many have hoped to contribute to research, others participated in studies related to their own health care, or, as has been claimed regarding Uighurs in China in one American lab, some may have been forced. The Today People are conceptually cast as past when geneticists perform a simple speech act of pronouncing them to be so. Thrown into relief, the ancestors take shape through inference and present-day scientific and human desires to explore through genes our as yet unknowable human history.

It is not possible to go back in time to sample our actual ancestors. Instead, the Today People are positioned within statistical models to stand in as proxies for them. This is not to say that inhabitants of Dublin, or Ibadan, or many other places do not share variation patterns in their DNA at different frequencies than groups elsewhere. The problem is the assumption that these patterns must have been inherited consistently from a source ancestral group long ago in a way that is more or less exclusive to the Irish or the Yoruba as they identify and are politically understood in name today. Instead, we know that the precolonial and colonial histories of the Irish, and of the people who now identify as Yoruba (but in most cases did not prior to the nineteenth century), are full of encounters with other groups where people mixed, merged languages, fused cultural practices, and, of course, shared DNA. Yet, when cast as parental, as static reference samples, their complexity—as humans living in a particular moment in history—dissolves into the shadows. They become silhouetted, absent presences known primarily for the geographical location geneticists would have them represent.

Fullwiley

In the early 2000s, some of the earliest iterations of autosomal testing grouped ancestors in terms of continental geography: one's ancestors were identified as being from Africa, Asia, Europe, and the pre-Columbian Americas. While subsequent tests have added nuances, such continental and sometimes national boundaries remain important features that structure how scientists differentiate ancestry groups as they seek to draw distinctions between minute fractions of specific populations' DNA markers. In so doing, and despite framing it in terms of sophisticated genetic probability and the seemingly neutral use of geographic divisions, geneticists' understanding of ancestry is heavily inflected by crude, yet persistent, ideas of race.

As reference datasets, the Today People are the backbone of ancestry DNA tests, and they are made to seem as though they are distant from people in places such as California, Wisconsin, or Massachusetts not only in space but also time. Yet, in reality, at least one highly researched group, consistently passed off as both distant and old, is really living right next door. Not unlike my neighbors up the road, they too claimed clear Western European roots and wore that badge in politically explicit ways.

These particular Today People reside just a few state lines away from me, in Utah. The Utah DNA was extracted from samples taken from Mormon families in Salt Lake City in the 1980s. The Mormons comprised the overwhelming majority of people used as part of a Paris-based international effort to create one of the first maps of the human genome starting in 1984. Scientists and Mormons shared the consensus that the Mormons were of Northern and Western European descent. Then they furthermore went on to become a global stand-in for "European"—specifically "Central European" (CEU)—in what would emerge as one of the most utilized genetic databases, used for myriad ancestry DNA tools, called the HapMap. Before the CEU peoples' inclusion in the HapMap in 2002, they were initially collected as a "Caucasian" panel of reference families for the French resource that stores, collects, and distributes diverse human genetic samples, the *Centre d'étude du polymorphism humain* (CEPH).

Today the Utah CEPH samples have again been repurposed for the 1000 Genomes Project and the International Genome Sample Resource Database. As concerns the latter, its website features a map of the world on which color-coded dots indicate where the genotyped sample populations come from. Curiously, the 2020 map contains no European or European-descended samples from the United States. Instead, the CEPH samples are placed on the map in France (presumably to represent "Central Europe"). The corresponding genomes, however, are called "Utah residents (CEPH)" with "Northern and Western European ancestry."

The CEU/CEPH humans are the perfect example of how genetic ancestry ideas are mashups of geography as well as assumptions about race and purity. That Mormon families were the bulk of the CEPH reference families is less surprising when one considers how their cultural emphasis on genealogy would have made them attractive to the original French team whose work was focused on "Caucasians." Here, a group obsessed with genealogical records and willing to be sampled aligned perfectly with the interests of scientists committed to a certain vision of race and who possessed the resources to widely broadcast the samples they collected. In the CEU/CEPH label, we witness one of the only times France has enshrined the United States, "Utah," as Old World. It is also one of the only times cosmopolitan Paris has proudly merged in an alliance of French *métissage* identity with Middle America. Salt Lake City as "Europe" thus became biologically entrenched, the locus of Western "Caucasian" ancestral roots, with the simple repurposing of the CEPH families for the initial HapMap and now its many afterlives.

The CEU Today People were the only samples representing Western Europe for the first two phases of the HapMap effort from 2002 to 2009. Crucially, this was a time when the initial ancestry testing technologies were being built in biomedical labs and in commercial sectors where individual ancestry kits were being devised for profit. 23andMe, DNA Print Genomics, Family Tree DNA, and countless others began offering DNA tracing tools to the public in the early to mid-2000s. Surely some companies had proprietary databases whose contents continue to be treated as trade secrets, yet many still relied in part on public samples that were widely shared.

Notably, the other "global populations" originally sampled for the HapMap were chosen, by contrast, from the actual geographic regions they were meant to designate historically. They are Han Chinese from Beijing (CHB), Japanese from Tokyo (JPT), and Yoruba from Ibadan (YRI). The most striking feature of this choice for many was that the HapMap was meant to be a resource that cataloged human diversity, and the groups were selected, in part, for the fact that they were European, Asian, and African.

Yet they were miniscule representations of the genetic diversity of each continent. Again, a narrow conception of human diversity—sectioned along present-day conceptions of race—appeared to be a fundamental aspect of the collection. And, of course, all were people from today's world.

If positioning our contemporaries as other, as old, as past has been the genius of the genetic genie of the ancestry testing industry, then the recurrent uses of the Utah samples for "Europe" cracks the genie's bottle—if only a bit. Time will tell if the move for companies to rightfully be more explicit and transparent about what belies their artful phrasings of ancestry will begin to shift perceptions. Recently, in an updated primer on how 23andMe ascertains what they call "ancestry composition," the company explained that most of their ancestral reference dataset is actually made up of contemporary people who pay to take their tests. The company writes:

> Customers comprise the lion's share of the datasets used by Ancestry Composition. When a 23andMe research participant tells us they have four grandparents all born in the same country—and the population of that country didn't experience massive migration in the last few hundred years, as happened throughout the Americas and in Australia, for example—that person becomes a candidate for inclusion in the reference data.

New Today People are growing this particular "ancestry" databases by the day. Meanwhile they are being massively repurposed for research into drug development through an exclusive agreement between

23andMe and UK-based pharmaceutical giant GSK. Their DNA, and its value, has again amplified.

FOR ANYONE INTERESTED in what these tests might provide them, it is important to keep in mind that the actual DNA taken from the reference samples are not full humans, with full genomes to be compared to testers' entire sequences. At-home tests analyze small quantities of human biological material that companies selectively compare to ours. "Ours" meaning those of us in the "New World," those seen to be fundamentally "mixed" in ways the ancestors—who are imagined to be more naturally pure (four grandparents born in the same country!)—are not. Direct-to-consumer testing is largely designed for the "mutts" of a modern history. This simultaneously puts consumers at the center of study while heralding a past devoid of "massive migration in the last few hundred years"—effectively suspending the reality that humans have mixed and moved throughout time.

The Us are the countless who come to testing for motives too numerous to catalog. For reasons tied to the violence of this country's colonization, many have no paper trail linking us to the varied strands of our origins. We can't get back the lands, kin, loves, and life that European colonialism and Western imperialism ripped away, leaving palpable societal and psychological traumas that mark our actual ancestors' descendants today. Our government has largely refused to entertain substantial Land Back requests of Native Americans, and refused to discuss the consistently tabled H.R.40, a bill to simply *consider* what reparations for U.S. slavery might entail. We cannot recuperate, even in these small gestures, what colonialism and racial bondage took. In light of these losses, ancestry testing itself may be a form of virtual restitution. A phantom of human remains handed back to the progeny since the much higher-value goods of countries, territory, lifeways, and lives themselves are out of the question for return.

We must ask, if many people actually desire the return of these things, then what work is commercial DNA testing actually doing? In some ways it recreates the past in a much more appealing tele-visual technicolor: a beautified, streamlined, open-ended cinematic landscape that can offer those dispossessed a slightly more palatable, if still haunted, human history. It evokes stories of profound human intrigue, of skin tones and facial features, of tribal names and exotic plains, of massive migrations and specifically named homelands. Any individual whose imagination is roused is invited to be part of familiar, romantic, and even tragically compelling scripts.

Humans are rightly moved by the perspectival lines and framed composition of ancestry painting. The reconstruction of one's ancestors inspires a feeling of largeness, of humanistic possibility. Understand-ably. Ancestry in these terms is art as science.

As a form of inventive expression molded by human hands, DNA ancestry shows that, culturally, science too contains multitudes—just like us, or our neighbors up the street.

TWO POEMS

Kyoko Uchida

(finalist for the Boston Review *Annual Poetry Contest)*

Breath

One.

The story goes:
      When Sun and Moon married
to people the string of seed pearl islands
as they'd seeded the sky with cold hard stars

after circling her husband to be
seven rotations mincing the hour,
the bride spoke first. Perhaps she merely said

Let me catch my breath. Yet because of her
breach of decorum, their first child was born
a leech, without limbs or vertebrae, just

a hungry mouth, was cast away from these
jade-green shores on a boat of woven reeds.
Seven times Moon circled a raging Sun

anew, kept quiet until he spoke first.
Their next child, the Sun Prince, descended from
the heavens to become our ancestor.

The End.
      And our leech-child sibling, exiled
to its mother's salty low tides? Teaching
itself to speak. Growing a spiky spine.

Two.

The word *son* is written as two *kanji*:
breath and *child*—the *kanji* for *breath* itself
composed of two characters: *self* and *heart*.

The word *daughter* is one *kanji* also
composed of two *kanji*: *woman* and *good*—
the same word as for any young woman:

a neighbor or a stranger, generic,
interchangeable. To be distinguished
only from *older sister* (*woman* and

Uchida

market), *younger sister* (*woman* and *end*),
bride (*woman* and *house*), *wife* (*woman* and *broom*),
or *old woman* (*woman under the waves*).

The character for *wife* also denotes
social position—a *lady* is *wife*
followed by *person*, ordinary wives

not being persons—or a profession:
nurse, cleaning woman, midwife, prostitute,
comfort woman.

Three.

    Written as three *kanji*:
Consolation—to master the heart; peace—
a woman under a roof; wife. There is

no consolation for those women whose
names we mispronounce, no peace even now,
no mastering a heart bound and gagged. For

the word accounts for no daughter, sister,
mother, not even a generic young
good woman. The word *ancestor* includes no

woman.

How is it that we're still learning
to draw breath, a lungful of burning coal
to speak, to name ourselves, our daughters?

From *Mother Tongues and Other Untravelings*

I have no sense of direction and it embarrasses my mother; she denies any family resemblance. I never learned to navigate, to translate forward motion into the pale grids of roadmaps, though as a child I'd loved the miniature geography of atlases and globes—for it was easy to know where the distant places were. It was where we were that I misunderstood. In a flashing maze of street names and storefronts, traffic circles, on- and off-ramps, I might remember a sharp left turn, or if the road curved as it climbed. What I don't understand is relative location, where each place is from where you are or where I've come from, how to articulate sequence of movement. I am here. You are there. I won't know the way back.

Down the wide gray corridor, we're leaving the hospital I hate. My mother is pregnant with my sister. I know, with no memory of her being big or slow-limbed, because she no longer holds my hand; I'm old enough, almost five. When we pass the kiosk with candy and magazines, I do not look longingly at the bright red tins of caramels. But as we come out into the blue November day, out of habit I reach up—and find a stranger's hand. Reeling with rage, I fly back down the corridor to the waiting room: green vinyl benches and slippered feet, canes, nurses' shoes, disinfectant stinging. She always said to wait by the exit if I got lost. *No running!* but I'm gone already, rounding the corner, nearly knocking into her.

Where have you been?

We say to each other as if in a game of mirrors.

I walked out with a stranger. I thought it was you.

It was *me. You were with* me.

I don't know why I mistook her for another, only how sure I was. I don't know if she's forgiven me, only that even then I'd delighted in my mistake, not knowing my mother or the girl who took her hand away and ran, motherless and nameless, back to her.

She writes on my birthday and at New Year's, otherwise rarely. I do not complain. My mother's letters come with boxes of food or clothes I do not need, are even more formal than my grandmother's.

A lesson in letter-writing: Begin with the greeting appropriate for the season: something different for mid-April and for late April, as the cherry blossoms fade and the leaves come in; for early and mid-June, as hues of green deepen with the plum rains. Assume the same weather for the other, that they are not far apart. Inquire after her health, even though you know already that she eats too little meat. Note the polite closing address to match the opening, the honorific after even a daughter's name.

Her briefest note has a beginning and an end, a sense that something substantial has been said. They come to me as postcards from a distant place of motherhood, written in a foreign tongue like weather we do not share. I recognize only the plainness of her signature, the abbreviated Chinese character for *mother* like a thumbprint seal.

THE MILLIONS
Deborah Taffa

IN NOVEMBER 2015 I boarded a flight to Peru with my husband Simone and a freshly broken arm. The trip was partly in response to a midlife crisis; that I would be doing it while nursing a broken bone felt fitting. I had rarely felt more in need of luck, or so short on it. While queuing in the airport terminal, I had asked the woman behind us if I could offer a sucker to her child. Giving candy to a child before every journey was a ritual I had observed since 1991, when a Senegalese marabout, a healer in Wolof society, told me I would spend a lifetime traveling and that the ceremony would help keep me safe. Call me superstitious, but I wasn't about to forego it now.

Breaking my arm only days before we were to leave— roller-skating, of all things—had meant a number of last-minute changes of plan. We scratched the grueling hike along the Inca Trail, and instead I had located a small hotel in T'oqokachi, the artsy San Blas district of Cusco. Still, it was a steep climb above the Plaza de Armas, at the center of town. Like many places in Peru, the Plaza de Armas has two names, one Spanish, one Indigenous: the other, Huacaypata, means "place of crying" in Quechua, which is fitting considering that the great revolutionary leader, Túpac Amaru II, was executed there in 1781.

Injured and not yet acclimated to the altitude, even the walk to the hotel from the bus station in the plaza was difficult. We rested after every block. My lungs burned. My arm ached. Our packs felt leaden. We sat outside the Temple of San Blas, a colonial church built on top of an Incan huaca dedicated to Illapa, the lightning god, for a rest. The view from the mountainside was stupendous, the valley stretching out beneath us in the late afternoon sun.

When we finally arrived at our temporary home, we were greeted by a middle-aged woman who said she was the owner. She spoke to us in rapid-fire Spanish, until she realized I wasn't keeping up. "I thought you were a local," she said, switching to English. I was flattered, watching as she flipped through our passports to check us in. After taking down our information, she handed our passports back and doubled down on her impression of me. "Your husband looks North American," she said. "But your dark hair fooled me."

I didn't want to be rude, so I held my tongue and, instead of saying anything, raised my eyebrow at Simone. He is from Milan, Italy, yet I was the one—with a thousand-year family history in the United States—who didn't fit her notion of what its citizens look like.

"I'm Native American," I explained, using the vaguest of terms to locate my ethnicity for her. I might have said that I was an enrolled member of the Quechan (Yuma) Nation, but making such a statement would undoubtedly have led to further questions, and once I started explaining, where would it end? Yes, *really*, I was born on the Fort Yuma Indian Reservation, but our name for ourselves is Quechan. No, *really*, we're not related to the Quechua of Peru, despite the fact that the spelling is very similar. In fact, we're from different linguistic groups entirely.

Once these facts were established, I would feel the urge to clarify that I am also Laguna Pueblo, because my grandmother was from Paguate, New Mexico, and she met my Quechan grandfather in Indian boarding school. I would explain that the U.S. government only allows Natives to enroll in one tribe, and finish by adding that my mother was born in Socorro, New Mexico, to mixed-race parents: part Indigenous and part Hispanic. My chattiness once I got started could be embarrassing, and it usually ended with me feeling like I had somehow overshared.

But, rather than asking The Question—"What tribe?"—or mentioning the existence of a Cherokee grandmother, the hotel owner said something I had never heard before, a statement that shocked me. She said, "You must be a millionaire! I mean, thanks to your casinos."

I was too tired to engage, and instead opted to shake my head and give a lighthearted laugh. There are 574 tribes in the United States alone. Few people realize that each has its own language, traditions, religious beliefs, and lifeways. My Quechan ancestors, for example, were water people, fishermen, and farmers, and wore their hair in river dreadlocks rather than braids. They came from the shores of the Colorado River, very close to where it rushed into the Gulf of California in the Sonoran Desert (before the building of so many dams). They were described by early explorers as a family of giants.

The Gulf of California divides my desert homeland in half: the states of Arizona (in the United States) and Sonora (in Mexico) to the east, and the Baja California Peninsula to the west. The surface area of the Gulf of California is the same size as the Sonoran Desert itself, which means our territory is half marine. My ancestors were born swimmers in the only North American desert that is also maritime. My ancestors also lost everything during the gold rush, when mining technology grew more sophisticated, and settlers began to prowl the state with greed. Despite federal efforts to uphold the signed treaties and protect Indigenous lands, the gold miners organized Sunday shoots in which white vigilantes would attack villages, killing as many people as they could in order to clear the land. The fact that I'm alive at all, given what my ancestors went through, feels like a statistical oddity escaped from a nightmare full of bleeding bodies in shallow graves.

But I didn't tell the hotel owner any of this. Instead Simone and I disentangled ourselves from her, took our keys, and headed to our room. Once inside, I sat on a chair while he helped me take off my boots. "Don't let her bother you," he said, knowing how a microaggression could spiral into a mood.

Our plan was to see low-lying archeological sites such as Pisac, until we became acclimated and could walk at high altitudes more easily. By the end of the first week we were feeling stronger and made our way to Qorikancha, the Inca's fifteenth-century Temple of the Sun in Cusco. Once gleaming with 700 gold-plated walls, altars, and statues, it was looted by the conquistadors, and bequeathed to Catholic Dominicans. The Spanish priests built the Santo Domingo convent, a blend of Andean and Spanish architecture, on top of and around Qorikancha. When a major earthquake struck in 1950, the chapel and bell tower of the convent were severely damaged. The 500-year-old mortarless stone of the Temple of the Sun, on the other hand, did not move, so superior was the engineering.

I first became interested in ancient cities in my teens, when I was attending high school in northwestern New Mexico. By then, I was angry, confused, and disgusted by the way my ancestors were spoken of as heathens. Unlike my own children, I was not guided through the thorns of history by educated parents. My mother and father were high school dropouts. They walked in silence, a silence that the United States was happy to confirm with gagged oral histories, government erasure, and the violence—both physical and ideological—of assimilation policies. Notable among these were the Indian boarding schools. Their legacy in my family would be hard to overstate; every subsequent generation operated with blindness at the center of its identity, until we started to do the hard work of recovering what can be.

Because Native representation was largely absent during my school years—because the truth about my people was not presented in my history classes—I felt ashamed. I hated the images that I did see of my people, sitting dejected and defeated in the dirt. I was alive but I was lesser. It's amazing what a child intuits even without being told. Terra nullius: the implication that my ancestors' way of existing on their land was inferior, that, like the bison and wild mustangs, we could be killed and deprived of our home to make room for others, that we were soulless and lacked the intellect or humanity to claim the mountains, valleys, and deserts that we loved.

Taffa

When I finally did find out about the gold rush, smallpox blankets, and massacres, the wars labeled as "skirmishes," the fight for civil rights amidst centuries of systemic racism, I was nearly an adult and the information poured in too suddenly. To this day, I wish I had learned it beside better news—that the doors to the past had been opened more empathetically, that alongside stories of calamity I had heard of joy in my lineage, that my people have also been botanists, philosophers, musicians, athletes, soldiers, designers, architects, and builders.

It was too painful to see my ancestors only as victims, and I began taking trips around the Southwest to camp and hike in Chaco Canyon, Mesa Verde, Canyon de Chelly, Aztec Ruins, and other architectural sites, where I could see their accomplishments on a grand scale. It was healing to walk through their ancient cities, and when I started having kids of my own in my twenties, I made a vow: they would learn about the stolen land and forced assimilation, but only in conjunction with visible signs of success.

This vow was the beginning of a long journey. We traveled to Mexico three times as a family in order to visit the Mayan cities of Chichen Itza, Tulum, Coba, Yaxchilan, Ek' Balam, Calakmul, and Palenque. We visited Anasazi ruins in our homeland, and drove to the ancient city of Cahokia in Illinois. We made these trips because I wanted my kids to gain an accurate picture of the skills, resources, and industry present in precontact America. I quoted Assata Shakur: "No one is going to give you the education you need to overthrow them. Nobody is going to teach you your true history, teach you your true heroes, if they know that that knowledge will help set you free."

I made my kids promise to be responsible for their own education, and to do the same if they had kids of their own.

As a result, three of our children beat me and Simone to Peru. They had returned home the previous summer raving about their experience. It was from them that I learned you could skip the touristic Inca Train to Machu Picchu by getting dropped at a hydro-electric station below Aguas Calientes. From this idea emerged the vision for the whole trip. I wanted to do like our children had done. Even after I broke my arm, I bargained with Simone: it was a short three-hour walk, nothing like the trek we had originally planned. He reminded me that the kids said they had to pass through a train tunnel quickly, and that you had to be ready to run.

Simone wouldn't back down; we ended up booking seats on the Inca Rail at the last minute. The tickets for the train were expensive, and then we were surprised to discover that our assigned cabins were in different cars despite being sequentially numbered. This is how I ended up sitting with three strangers. One, a young white woman, had come to Peru to heal herself by taking the entheogen plant medicine ayahuasca. Ayahuasca is made from the giant woody liana vine. Brewed with other plants, it is served as a tea that is meant to access the divine within.

"How did you find your *curandero*?" I asked. My question prompted a whole story. She was traveling with her father, who had also been seated in another car, and she was upset that his experience with the psychedelic medicine had been more fruitful than her own. Part of me felt cynical about her hiring a curandero—a shaman, or medicine man, or whatever she wanted to call him. She was a spiritual tourist. She admitted she had reached out to him online, before launching into a long confession that took the bulk of the trip. Her mother had died, and the loss had damaged her for years. At first her father had tried to discourage her focus on non-Western medicine, but the more she educated him about the healing properties of ayahuasca, the more she could see that he was changing his mind until finally he had agreed to travel with her.

She spoke about the grueling nature of the ceremony, how many of the participants had thrown up and cried. It was challenging, an opportunity for growth, but she had missed it. She had clenched her eyes and refused to open them. She refused to surrender to the medicine, while her father had visions and was praised by the curandero for being a genuine seeker. According to her account, her father had come away from his experience with a feeling of infinite love, while she had felt nothing.

Her experience of the ceremony was quite opposite my own experiences in the Native American Church where I had taken grandfather peyote four times in my twenties. It was a profoundly healing experience for me, yet one that I could only imagine partaking in because of my intimacy with cacti and the desert. Reciprocity sits at the heart of Indigenous medicine, and a person's intent when taking power plants determines the results. As I listened to her speak, I reflected on the West's poor track record with appreciating Indigenous practices. I wanted to tell her I would never waltz into the jungle and pay someone to provide me with ayahuasca. For me it would feel necessary to see the jungle first, walk through her, and see if she invited me. The ceremonies I have taken part in always involved a chance encounter and invitation I didn't overtly seek.

Thankfully, I said nothing. She was earnest, visibly wounded, disappointed by her missed opportunity and what she saw as a lack of courage at the ceremony. We pulled into the station, descended the steps of the train, and said goodbye. I stood on the platform by myself until Simone arrived and I told him about the woman and her experience. I heard myself preaching: Westerners had much to gain from Indigenous people, but why couldn't they see that, for everything received, something had to be given?

As I was speaking, an Incan busker walked by, and in a kind of out-of-body experience, I momentarily saw myself through his eyes, an American animatedly holding forth in a heavily touristed train station.

I saw that many people came to the Inca homeland wanting the past to heal present wounds, hoping that some form of ancient wisdom might seep through the cracks of our twenty-first-century existence to make them feel less alone. And I was one of them, here in this bustling international crowd. In that moment, I felt less Indigenous and more like a tourist with a powerful passport. Meeting the woman on the train—witnessing her eagerness as a wounded tourist—made me consider my own strategy for healing. She was there seeking Indigenous wisdom in a way that centered my cultural lens. At the same time, I was there valorizing Indigenous grandeur, and it somehow revealed the depth of my fracturing. Is "civilized society" synonymous with kings and empires, subjects and vast cities? If the logic of colonization was, "Indigenous people are not using the land, therefore we're taking it," what happened in the centuries that followed? Now that the land has been "put to good use," where do we find ourselves? The land has been abused, and now we find ourselves on the verge of collapse.

I wondered how many of the other tourists churning through the station came, at least in part, because they too were injured and confused and wanted to partake in the wisdom of yesteryear in order to get through today. Could I blame them? Perhaps they needed ancient beliefs, practices, and traditions just as I had needed Western medicine to set my broken arm.

As if to remind me of this, my wrist ached as we hiked from the train station up to the Sun Gate. Yet I felt contentment at my revelation and chatted with strangers who paused to ask what had happened to my arm. I had never felt more united with a crowd in my life. What did I have in common with them? And what did I have in common with ancient Incans? These were questions that ran through my mind for days.

My questioning reached its peak a couple of days later while visiting the regional history museum in Cusco. We would soon be heading to Lima and from there home, and I remained curious about Túpac Amaru II, the executed Incan noble whose death was mourned so profoundly that it still gave name to the square. Of him I knew little, though. I knew that his American Revolution had taken place thirty years before ours in the United States, and that the Spanish Crown, which wanted to continue plundering the riches of its American colony, had viciously killed him in the plaza, as it previously had his great-grandfather and namesake.

In the museum, we learned that he and his wife, Micaela, inspired a three-year revolution that spread throughout Peru and

Bolivia, terrifying stakeholders in Madrid. A descendant of both Inca nobility and influential Spanish conquistadors, Túpac Amaru II was born José Gabriel Condorcanqui. Educated by Jesuits, he spoke both Quechua and Spanish and was recognized as a *kuraka*, or Incan spiritual authority and tax collector. Túpac and Micaela owned land, but they also had many debts. His travels brought him in contact with Indigenous and mestizo peasants. He saw their suffering and strategized with Micaela to help improve their lives. They filed applications with authorities in Tinta, Cusco, and Lima in order to free their poor brethren from forced labor in Peruvian mines. Authorities resisted them, however, and they came to despise the entire encomienda system as a result.

The encomienda system was a Spanish colonial caste hierarchy in which Spanish-born citizens held the highest positions, even if their families back home were uneducated. Being born in America, no matter how important your family, destined you to lower status. Mestizos (people of mixed European–Indigenous heritage) were in the middle, and at the very bottom were Indians and Africans, both seen as expendable laborers.

After repeated failures in the courts, Túpac and Micaela abducted an important Spanish politician, Antonio Arriaga, and hanged him in front of a crowd of Incans, mestizos, creoles, and "good" Spaniards. This act of war began a military campaign in which they demanded the abolition of slavery, the repeal of taxes known as the "king's tenth," the restitution of ancestral lands, and legal authority for women. Their goal was ultimately to create an Indian-Mestizo-Creole nation as well as a return to Incan ways. They ransacked haciendas and textile mills, gathering allies as they moved south through Peru. In 1781, after 100,000 war fatalities, they failed to take the city of Cusco and were captured.

Although they did not succeed in taking the seat of power, their politics instilled a new state of mind in South America, encouraging Incans and other tribes to join forces with mestizos and creoles, since they all shared a single oppressor. Thus their war lived on. Because of their fighting efforts, an Indigenous nationalism spread through southern Peru, Bolivia, and Argentina.

Túpac and Micaela never saw the fruit of their liberation ideology, how their story still affects Indigenous people today. The museum emphasized how brutal their deaths were at the hands of the Spaniards. Micaela was forced to watch the hanging of her son. Túpac begged for Micaela's life, and when his prison guards would not give him paper and a pen to write her a final letter, he used his own blood on his clothing to record his misery. The day after their son's death, he was forced to watch Micaela be strangled to death before being quartered and beheaded himself, his body parts dumped in loyal villages as a warning. Their family land and gardens were strewn with salt, and documents confirming their descent were destroyed. A law was passed that made self-identification as an Incan illegal, and all Incan clothing and cultural traditions were banished.

Through the pain of their story, I vowed to never again question whether I had something in common with the Inca, or anyone else who stood for healing against antidemocratic forces. Democracy *is* Indigenous, and against the baseline assumption to think of the history of the United States as a story told east to west (the forward march of a valiant people on their way to tame the wild frontier), I knew that was the wrong axis to tell my story. It was instead my responsibility to see the Americas north to south, to recognize what Túpac had tried to convey with his final breath. After seeing his loved ones die, after losing his wife and revolutionary companion, knowing pain and death awaited him, he defied those in power before the executioner cut out his tongue by saying, both in Quechua and Castillian: "I will be back and there will be millions of us." My family back home, the tourists at Machu Picchu, Indigenous people around the world, a quarter of the planet in number but too often separated by manmade borders, we were his vision of now.

As we left the museum to head back to our hotel, I thought about the desert people from whom I came. Their houses simple wickups made of palm leaves, the open desert with nary a grand castle except for those created by a superior mirage, and for the first time I felt proud that my ancestors had walked lightly on the land. The difference between an empire and a meaningful community is the mental and physical health of the individual.

When I returned home after the trip, I learned that my wrist had set off center. It was a fitting discovery. I have come to know that healing never restores us to the way we were before getting hurt. Being injured leads to permanent changes in our bodies and our psyches. Even the way I raised my kids, so careful to have them avoid the injuries of my own youth, began with a distortion of my own making. To live in this world is to perpetually seek balance from imbalance as we try to heal wounds that result from a cavernous divide.

Taffa

TWO POEMS

Diamond Forde

(finalist for the Boston Review *Annual Poetry Contest)*

The Third Book of Alice Called
LAWS

Laws 3:1   **Pig Feet and Black-Eyed Peas**

Her knife knuckles   between the toes,   splits
an onion, phosphorescent   sliver of the moon,
peas twice soaked   and boiling, bay leaf   and bell
pepper,   bouillon, salt, the whole house
smellin' like down-home   grease and garlic,
procreant stank on the stove,   Alice knows
hunger, its costumes—tight-belly-tweed-
   hunger,   orgasms in organza, even
       the cotton-mouthed hunger of home.
Beans blink in the pot. Trotters split their sinew, sigh.
Upstairs, her husband's brother
duets with Otis,   try a little tenderness, a two-step
shuffles down, stirs   kids from their beds.
She will mother them
       the way she once was mothered: psalms still wet
in her smile, each kiss   a map back—Alice throws
the window open, and heat carries
         the sweet stink of miles to the borough.

The second Alice's Studebaker stuttered from the lot to the night service, where the gospel choir paddled through tidal couplets of piety and prayer, the daughters, back home, nosed a needle over the forbidden record their cousins smuggled in under their shirts.
2 Rhythm and blues, the tunes Alice banned with the first man. If Alice could've seen the house tinseled with Martha & The Vandellas, the Isley Brothers filigreed on the rug, Betty Everett dittied about the girls' room—
3 And the cousins circled around the floor length mirror, their shirts tied, checkered and paisley button-ups bonneting their midriffs
4 Then the daughters, too, the whole girl-gaggle flicking their otter bodies to the guitar's pulse, wanting hips and a boy with hands capped like a minaret against them.
5 This, till a voice creaked from the stairwell, their brother, lookout for the pecan-colored putter of Alice's jalopy plunking up the drive. Then the music stopped. The evening quieted back in.

2 Once, while the daughters danced in their room, the youngest daughter crawled away to taste each splintered offering of her home world: the mango-sweetness of a dining set, cambric brillo of an ottoman pressed against the gums, then beneath the sink, the daughter gulped the roach spray, its alarming whiteness bubbling at the corners of her mouth until, finally, she was found.
2 Then the daughters, afraid to tell Alice she might've missed the preamble to her youngest daughter's death, stopped the music, untied their shirts, fell to their knees to pray.

3 But the youngest daughter didn't die that day and by sunrise was well enough to nub the blue end of a plastic schooner toy between her budding teeth
2 But the daughters were done with mirrors

3 But I wish I could take them back to the gyre and jive of discovering they are the sunrise blotting Monet's blue wharf. My momma among them, too young to dance, but old enough to believe love was something never meant for her.
4 Our bodies, temples—shouldn't that mean anyone can worship? Shouldn't that mean it's okay to dip my hips into a communion bowl?

4 I confess I was nearly twenty before I could touch myself the first time, trembling like a weaverbird against the tightly woven nest in my chest.
2 Finally, I understood my below as more than blood home, as more than a hard week on a basement floor hooded around a portable heater, the blade edge of a streetlight scything in to find me praying the heater's molten glow would ooze through, burn brighter than the white-hot pain of a uterus cauliflowered by tumors
3 And the first time I tried to die was because of this—because I couldn't sum my body beyond its function, its nettled, needled pins.
4 What I would have done for a toe hair ode, a uterine elegy, a ballad of lopsided breasts—any body-warble louder than the ache barking inside me.

5 I'm so tired of my body—afraid of what I don't know about it, that if I stop writing I might become that girl again, on the bedroom floor, loathing a muscle-clench, my detached blood a hermit crab in molt.
2 I'd love to shed my skin, to emerge new and pink-gleaming, reach for the old pearlescent shell of my elbows, for my pebbled knees, for the dimple in my chin puckered to nurse.

MEDITATIONS ON LINES
Felicia Zamora

Water takes the path of least resistance. Any competent plumber spouts this tried & true logic. Water disobeys. Water wants what water wants. Water claims & claims. If you live in the desert long enough, you become watchful of water. Water makes up 83% of lungs; 74% of brain & heart. Tuning fork of organs. Protective. Even, our watery bones. You meet the saguaro & touch your clavicle in kinship. What you can lug around. How roots tendril inside a body. You wonder how long before the spikes & spindles evolve you.

))))   ((((

Before I was a cell, I was a whisper of a cell from another cell. A longing.

))))   ((((

Our fingers between the chain-link fence. Our silhouettes cast into pool before our bodies. Water glistens mercury in moonlight. Our skinny limbs under layers peeling onto cement. Under the diving board, you enter me, up to knuckles. My frame squirms in the chlorine. You bring your finger to your nose. "You don't smell like a dirty taco." & I see muscles constrict along your shoulder blades, your frame pulls out of the wet.

))))   ((((

Count 499 seconds: the time for light to leave the sun & hit earth. About eight minutes. We label this number one; one Astronomical Unit. We define. & from our definitions, causality in abundance. The psychologist duo Dr. Susan Fiske & Dr. Shelley Taylor coined us *cognitive misers*. Our brain tendrils & pathways not unlike water, in search of facile, of ease. Why scale the redwood when the stream carries our bulbous bodies in gentle sway?

))))   ((((

Nothing about the human body suggests effortlessness.

))))   ((((

After the plumber augers the main sewer line, he stands on the basement steps & says, "You seem like clean people," & continues his story about a slumlord who "had 15 Latinos living in a basement knee-deep in feces." He groans a chuckle. My organs flinch & my cells swell. My ears fill; I'm fifteen again under water, lungs in burn & his voice muffles away as I sink further below surface.

))))   ((((

Zamora

Perhaps Fiske & Taylor got it wrong; the body made to *act in*, suggesting environment & in turn, *be acted upon*, suggesting relationship. We define to feel whole. We define to use the tongue & teeth & mandible & epiglottis to construct home in a language full of gaps; a language that, at times, despises us. Lungs & throat & air swirl & a voice emerges. Amiri Baraka said, "Context . . . is most dramatically social."[1] Our definitions fail in the linear. Think of the zigzags, the rounded curves of any context filtered through veils of haze in our hippocampus. Did we forget the circulatory systems of veins, arteries, vessels, & nerves twisting inside of us?

))))   ((((

Maggots collect in a tiny inlet of plastic filled with water after 22 hours of rain. Half of the cream, cylindrical bodies float, still. The other half writhe & circle the dead. If design exists here, Frost, what horrid spell cast.

))))   ((((

Light bends by itself. In 94.36 million miles, the sun's rays reach our pupils. Any physics textbook tells us light travels in a straight line. Yet, we now know light bends by itself. Light travels in curves without external influence.

))))   ((((

Our walking circuitous solar systems under flesh.

))))   ((((

A lesson in windows. Corneas hold the power of refraction; the cornea bends rays through the pupil to enter us. The face: a camera & our irises: shutters. Collection built in our compositions. Ciliary muscles mold the lens's shape, bend here flatten there, to focus light & images on the retina. The rods & cones of us in photoreceptive cells. How a definition bends to desired shape. Fenestrae in the brain, in the lungs, the throat. Open the transom. Breathe.

))))   ((((

Women develop complete sets of cells. I develop from ovum living inside my mother's ovary while inside my grandma's womb. I begin immature cell from immature ovum inside a womb. I am a woman of a woman of a woman. Interior ghost in haunt.

))))   ((((

You take me to the edge of nothing. No longer palimpsest for your butchery. I wring my shins & torso & spine & forearm; collect my own fluids. Drink.

---

[1] From Amiri Baraka's essay "Expressive Language."

Zamora

ANCESTRAL WEALTH:
THE SACRED BLACK MASCULINE IN MY LIFE
Tyehimba Jess

I CAN'T HIT THE PAGE without hearing Hendrix, his psychedelically blued guitar journeys I bathed in for at least an hour every day for four or five years of my early twenties until I'd memorized every solo, him fingering feedback and folding wah wah into sonic ambulances of soul. I can't hit the page without the echo of Muddy Waters's Mississippi guitar that found its way to an electrified Chicago, without hearing the "I'm a Man" foundational blocks with his legendary harmonica men—Little Walter, Carey Bell, James Cotton, Junior Wells, Big Walter Horton, George Smith. I hear their tremolo and bravado, the shuffles, train tracks and galactic howls seeping from their mouths through reeds and between their fingers, and I ache to bring it to the page—I bleed to breathe it into stanzas. I can't hit the page without Yusef Lateef and John Lee Hooker and Curtis Mayfield blazing across the chorus. I can't hit the page without Prince on stage at the Super Bowl strutting in the rain, singing his signature into the far-off lightning. I can't hit the page without Al Green's falsetto grinding against his acoustic guitar, making the angels grit their teeth with jealousy. I can't hit the page without Coltrane walking the bar with his horn, scraping the blues into abstraction from beneath a heated spoon. I can't hit the page without Art Tatum's cataracted cosmic vision burning up the eighty-eights with blinding speed. I can't hit the page without Mingus and Diz and Marley and Fred McDowell and Howlin' Wolf whisper-growling in my ear to know their names with mine.

I can't hit the page without Amiri Amiri Amiri Amiri Amiri Amiri Amiri. I heard the Lightnin' Hopkins, the Sun Ra, the Ellington and Basie and Ayler he firestormed to the stage when he roared and laughed and proclaimed. I can't hit the page without Langston Hughes in one pocket, Ernest Gaines in another and Leon Forrest on the nightstand. I can't hit the page without James Baldwin and August Wilson on the passenger side with Sam Greenlee in the back talking shit and all us laughin'.

Many so many of them were not always gentlemen or gentle men. Many so many of them were imperfect, flawed, at times dangerous, needy, selfish, and small. Many so many of them were many times intractable and stubborn, peevish and rude. Rambunctious. Troublesome. Inappropriate. Wrong. But when they put their demons down, or even tricked those demons to help pick up their swords of imagination and will to help do the dirty lovely Black Sorcery of Fully Being, they were doing service to the business for which they were sent to this planet. And many so many of them have taught me nobility with the words unsaid or the truth laid just so. And many so many of them have split themselves open with sacrifice when nobody was watching. And many

Jess

so many of them took it and took it and never threw back in spite. And many so many of them were larger than anything they'd ever imagined and propped multitudes on their shoulders, King-like, with Malcolm defiance, or just by safeguarding their families' homes.

They knew that being BLACKMANINAMERICA™ means to always be under suspicion. To embody the bullseye of an American tradition that no other demographic has been so thoroughly tied to—being tied to a tree by a throbbing, festive mob and then castrated, whipped and burned alive like a torch lighting up the country's cavernous carnivorous heart. That more than any other demographic, they could be accused of the unthinkable with no evidence and forced to pay with life or years of life. These men realized that there is no way out of the maelstrom, but that there was a way into themselves that no one else could fully capture or own—their voices playing out on microphones or keyboards or finger pads or strings or drums or even through a tiny pencil in a tiny cell staring at forty-seven pictures taped to a wall. And to speak from that kind of will, that kind of pigheaded hope, strutting ambition and desire to know yourself through pure expression is a kind of love. A love that just might turn a life around and that a man can build a life around.

I couldn't hit the page without my homefolk like Detroiter Dudley Randall, who told me once just before I left the D for good that maybe writing was what I needed to do. I couldn't hit the page without another native Detroiter, Haki Madhubuti, whose tracks I followed to Chicago and whose bookstore was the first Black-owned bookstore I'd ever bought a book from—Dudley Randall's *The Black Poets* anthology.

And I couldn't hit the page without another Detroiter, Robert Hayden, who peered through his coke-bottle glasses and, so some tell me, would sometimes cry when he'd ask the question, *What do I know of love's austere and lonely offices?*

What *do* I know of love's austere and lonely offices?

I loved it when Miles turned his back to the audience—'cause I knew that he was about to play *his* liberation and not buck for the crowd. I loved it when Muhammad Ali asked Ernie Terrell over and over the question that would define his life—"What's my name?"—and pounded each syllable of his identity into America's TV sets. I loved it when Walter Payton bulldozed and ballet-danced his way across end zones 'cause I knew he was running toward greatness, weaving through obliteration with every yard. I loved it when Richard Pryor laughed against his smoked-up demons, when Redd Foxx told me to wash my ass. I love Mingus about as much as I love the austerity of Sterling Plumpp's poems that taught me how the blues still lives in our stories; about as much as I love the flare in Sammy Davis's tap dance and the moondust in Michael Jackson's walk; about as much as I love the loneliness in Marvin Gaye's falsetto; about as much as I love the lushness of Charles White's paintings and Romare Bearden's collages.

I know the austerity of my father's love—that it is hard and thorny like a stubborn, starved weed. I don't know the loneliness of being born in 1929 and growing up Black in Greenville, South Carolina, in the dead weight of America's Depression. I don't know the austere loneliness of my

Jess

grandfather who was drafted in World War II despite having three kids to support, but I think I know a bit of the Withers in his deep silences that he passed down to my father. I don't know the kind of austerity that was branded onto my dad between southern lynchings and northern segregation, and I can only imagine his loneliness navigating to Detroit and a PhD in chemistry by age twenty-seven. I don't know the austerity of raising a family in the seventies and eighties, and I only know of his loneliness now when he calls me from Detroit after months in quarantine, eager to show the love he'd hidden for so many years like a secret bank account with passcodes he can barely remember. But I know that I can't hit the page without him either—that it was his newspapers, magazines, and books that I was reading for fun as a kid in my first library, that I wish I had his level of sheer concentration when he studied or read, that I still have some of his stubborn nature when it's hard for me to tell him "I love you."

I can't hit the page without all of them, all the pages and pages of Black men I could mention here that whispered or screamed in my ear with the same desire to live honestly free. *All* these brothers, uncles, daddies, and pops—the sinners and the soulsters and the saints alike. I can't hit the page without hearing them at my elbow or in my ear, even when they fuck up terribly and even when I'm tryin' not to envy how brilliant they be. You see, as Etheridge once told me, *I know their style, they know mine. I am all of them, they are all of me.*

—

Note: *The phrase "Sacred Black Masculine" is from Dr. T. Hasan Johnson's ruminations on the subject in the development of Black Male Studies.*

SKYLARKING
Racquel Goodison

THE SECOND TIME Auncil's picture appeared in the *Gleaner*, his mother blocked his path with her big body. She tried preventing him from riding his beloved bike, even if just with friends. Every time she noticed he was dressed for sport, she'd head for the door.

Auncil hated this new obstacle to the world outside his home and hated even more the accompanying lectures about the dangers of life. He was already twenty-one. He did not need to hear her sighs and grumbles, her saying, "I don't know why you have to live so. You must want me go to a' early grave. A that you want? Eeh?"

"Why you have to carry on so?" he'd sigh. And, his father might add, "Make the boy go have some fun, Dorcas." But they knew it came down to getting past her and it would take some doing.

"Why you cyaan stay as you yard, Auncil? Why you love to gallivant so?" she'd press.

"I have to live me life, mama! I can't stay in the house like some rat. A that you want fi me?"

"I don't know why you ha' fi go bout so much, is all. . . . You is everything to us, you know."

"I know, mama," he'd say. *But oonu get to decide on that. What me get to choose?* he'd think and never once say out loud.

He would feel a stabbing pain in his chest as his annoyance rose but he could not bring himself to argue too much with her. She meant so much to him. It would hurt even more than his annoyance to do anything as feisty as talk back, even at his age—especially at this age. Instead, he'd put a smile on and hug her tight. She would sigh again, this time into his shoulder—he was that much taller than her—and then beg him, as he walked out, "Please, I beg you, don't kill me today with any foolishness."

By foolishness he thinks she meant chances with his life, as if he was not a top-ranked cyclist known for his deft skills during the steep downhill street races that sometimes happened in the hills of St. Andrew. On the front page of the *Gleaner* he'd appeared in his striped bicycle shorts and shirt and matching cap, his legs still on the pedals as if he was in mid-cycle. What chances did she think he was taking? And today? Did he even look as if he was going racing?

He felt good in his new clothes that he had bought with his last winnings. From the baby blue bush jacket to the dark blue polyester pants, everything was brand new and crisp. And though his white leather shoes were not new, they had been polished to an even brighter shine than the day he had seen them in the store. Anybody with eyes could see that Auncil was going out on the town.

He was heading out to take the Sunday morning train from Kingston to Montego Bay. It was the end of his last free summer, that special time between his recent graduation from the university and the beginning of his life as a professional man. A time that was an ending and a beginning. He had raced every chance he could and made a decent amount of change, enough to help his parents a bit and to also give himself some spending money before his "free paper bu'n." He had earned this break, this summer, and this day out.

Auncil was not about beating the clock when he went out the door. Today he was about skylarking and did not need his mother to try to make him feel bad about having a little life while he could.

At the train station, he tugged on the hem of his shirt and smiled at the thought of seeing Benson and Nigel again. He had met them in first form of high school and they had become fast friends. They were all bookish boys who were obsessed with ska and soccer. Benson and Nigel had lived with their respective aunties while they went to school in Kingston and were as serious about their grades as Auncil was. Their futures were tied to their families' well-being as much as it was to their own. Any failure would be beyond some personal disappointment. They were all only children as well and it was as if their circumstances had made them brothers, the best of bredrens from the minute they'd met.

After their A-levels, they had parted ways only so far as miles go. Auncil had gone on to the University of the West Indies. Benson had gotten a job with the bauxite mining corporation near his mother's house in St. Ann, and Nigel was teaching at a secondary school in Manchester where his folks lived. The miles did nothing to diminish their connection, however. They wrote often and sometimes they would find a way to spend some time together, like they used to, if either Auncil went to the north coast of the island or they came to

Kingston. It had been over a year since he had seen them last though because he had been so busy studying and then racing to fund his one last relatively free summer.

AUNCIL LOOKED AROUND at the rest of the crowd waiting for the train. There were more people there than he thought there would be even on this Sunday. Many more. But it should have been expected. For months the Holy Name Society of St. Ann's Roman Catholic Church had been advertising the day trip from Kingston to Montego Bay. It was in the paper, on the radio, and all over the streets in conversations and fliers: "A day to remember! A bashment of the best sort! Wear your best and come celebrate the last weekend of the summer of '57! Come one! Come all!!"

Auncil had, of course, seen and heard and even talked about this trip, but he was not a church man and between studying for his exams to qualify as an accountant and finally completing his degree so he'd be set for life—life as a working man who could support his parents—he had not thought much about buying a ticket or about the fact that his day trip was on the same day as this grand affair. It had been a long road to this summer and—with his father no longer able to support him and his mother since his hands got too stiff to make shoes—Auncil wanted more than anything to finally get the piece of paper, that degree, that would set him on his way to adding to the household instead of still being one more expense to manage, one more future barely hanging in the balance.

All around him the sun bounced off the bright clothing of the hundreds of people dressed to the nines: the plump light brown girl in the yellow polka-dot dress and green patent leather shoes; the man in his crisp beige short-sleeve shirt and matching pants with a crease so sharp it looked like it was made of something harder than cloth; the children dressed as if they were going to Christmas service instead of a day in Mo'Bay.

Auncil felt the sweat trickle from the top of his head. He was wearing a straw hat with a small brim, but the heat of this last weekend of August reminded him they were still in the midst of hurricane season. Not even his finely made hat could combat this weather. As he swiped the sweat from his brow, he felt the wind announce the approach of the train and soon also heard it chug along the tracks and roll to a stop for all to board. The train, like so much of this day, was spruced up: a new diesel engine and extra cars for the bigger crowd. To Auncil, all things about this day seemed new and built for better times.

The ride to Mo'Bay was smooth, the crowds tightly packed but convivial. Someone hummed "Nearer My God to Thee" and Auncil thought briefly of his father who would sing hymns when he used to shape the shoes over the wooden molds he stored in the zinc shed behind the house. As a child, Auncil used to sit on the concrete steps and watch his father work like some kind of artist. He was a tall man who was darker than Auncil and he did not speak much. But, still, Auncil felt a warmness watching him work. "You good, my star?" he'd sometimes ask. "Make sure you study them books and get a job with you head. Don't want to end up a manual laborer like this ol' man."

Goodison

Auncil had heard this time and time again, but he saw no problem with this kind of work. In fact, he wished his father would take him on and show him how he made such beautiful shoes, shoes sought after by enough people to pay his school fees and provide a goat at Easter. Instead, he studied like they wanted and got top marks. He became a scholarship boy and now he was a college graduate. It had been a long journey of many nights bent over books. Many years of one high-stakes exam after another. Now, he could begin to reap the rewards. Just in time.

His father's fingers had turned to stiff yams, like something someone dug up from the ground, turgid and twisted. The chickens they raised were rationed and mostly for eggs, and his mother was now sewing day and night to keep even a little rice in the house. Watching her bent over the Singer sewing machine, pedaling past midnight, was enough to make Auncil study even harder than he had in high school. For a time, the only socializing and fun he let himself have was when he raced down those steep hills, no hand-brakes, no padding, no helmets. Just the wind rushing over his face and arms, the burn in his chest and legs, the tears from the pain and the joy—and the feeling that he was faster than even his own thoughts, more able and glorious than he often dared to hope.

His mother, though, did not know about the racing until that photograph had appeared in the *Gleaner*. Auncil had won another race and some journalist had rushed up and taken a picture of him still on his bike. He'd asked Auncil for his name and, knowing that his mother would not approve of such reckless skylarking, he had told him a made-up one. He did not think the photo would appear in the national paper. But it had. And, even with the fake name, of course his mother found out where he sometimes went on Saturday mornings. The way she carried on, you would have thought he had become a drug addict or a madman or a murderer. For weeks after the discovery, she would mumble, as if to herself but clearly within his earshot, "See me dying trial? Oonu see it? De lawd know say trouble don' set like rain. . . ." His father just sat on the same steps that Auncil used to watch him from and sipped milk and white rum while staring at the zinc shed.

They could not know how that wind, that speed, that sense of flying and having legs like pistons kept him from utter despair at the sight of what their lives had become. They could not seem to see how those races and the victories made him feel that he could do anything.

THE FIRST TIME Auncil's photo appeared in the paper was a day his parents would never forget. Patrick and Dorcas had been married for six years by the time that day arrived. Before Dorcas was seen walking home from the hospital with the tiny bundle in her arm, she had had other pregnancies that ended with dead babies. Too poor to get a car ride and weak from the delivery a mere two days earlier, she walked like she was being carried home, back straight, smile wide, and feet quick. Patrick walked beside her and hoped that everyone they passed could witness the boy God had given him. He was pleased to grant permission when a photographer from the paper who was charged with taking pictures of newborns for possible publication with cute captions snapped a picture of Auncil swaddled in his blanket.

As was the case with the second, more recent photo, no one thought that baby picture would get published. In fact, no one thought of it again until it was discovered in the paper days later: "Auncil Thomas arrived on the scene ready to take hold!" He was round and pale, cheeks like puffed-up coco bread, and gripping the finger of someone who was out of the frame.

When Auncil's mother saw the racing photo, she could not help but remember that moment so soon after he was born and wonder how many times her baby would end up in the news.

WHEN AUNCIL ARRIVED at his destination, Benson and Nigel were easy to spot. Both were over six feet tall, like Auncil, and while one was pale to the point of appearing luminescent in the sun, the other was so dark it seemed that even the island's sunshine was swallowed by the depth of his skin's shade. Auncil was glad to see them.

It was as if he were back at Ardenne High School, just a boy once more with nothing to worry about but passing his exams, finding time for soccer after school, and hoping that some girl he found attractive would like him back.

Auncil had spent the first moments at Ardenne wondering if he could make a space for himself there. Would he find friends? Would he be smart enough? Would he be able to keep his grades up and hang on to his scholarship? Was he, in fact, worthy? Enough?

He knew the price of his parent's poverty. He knew that they had not had his luck. They had not been able to go further than primary school and had had to find some skill they could live off and use to help support their family by the time they were fifteen. He knew he had to succeed.

In his home room, they placed the students in alphabetical order. In front of him was Benson Singer and, behind him, Nigel Thornhill. When the bell rang for recess, the three boys had walked out into the yard in the same order they had sat all morning.

"You buying lunch?" Benson had been the first to speak.

Nigel and Auncil turned at the same time and looked at him. Auncil held up the ham sandwich wrapped in brown paper just as Nigel explained that his aunty had packed him leftover curried chicken and white rice. And, like so, they had found each other.

Auncil saw it as another stroke of luck. He would not be alone in this school full of kids who probably had more money and intelligence than he was born with. He might just have enough to get through the work of staying afloat in this new river to cross.

After he had gotten into high school, his mother had quickly made all his uniforms. She washed and pressed them weeks before the start of the first term, then hung them on some nails his father had hammered, just for this purpose, into a wall of Auncil's tiny bedroom. Sometimes Auncil would wake up to his mother standing quietly in front of the uniforms, watching them. Sometimes she carefully touched a sleeve or a button.

The morning he set out for his first day of high school, she made him his favorite breakfast, mackerel and boiled green bananas. As he ate, she watched him and smiled. When he was done and was licking his fork, she said, still smiling but with a serious note in her voice, "The hard work just beginning now, Auncil. Don't get complacent." She said this after every hurdle he cleared. Each time it made his stomach hurt and his heart speed up.

So, it was no small thing that he had encountered two classmates who were willing to literally walk with him from day one. By the end of his first recess with his new friends, he felt more assured. They had even gone so far as to share each other's meals and make plans to kick around Nigel's soccer ball after dismissal. It felt like a Godsend.

NOW, during that Sunday in Mo'Bay, Auncil told them about his graduation and the new job he would start. Benson told them about his engagement to a very pretty girl from his church. And Nigel told them about the promotion he was hoping to get.

"T'ings a look good fi we!" Nigel announced as he took a drink of some beer from a bottle.

"A true, I-ya. A true. . . ." Auncil agreed. "Me just hope say mi parents don' create problems when me start fi make moves."

Benson burst out laughing, "You can g'waan hope, bredda! None a we parents know how fi leave a man in peace!"

Auncil and Benson nodded and chuckled. Then they fell into silence for a while, each one appearing to drift into his thoughts. Soon enough, their reunion was over and it was Auncil's time to return to Kingston.

He hoped his mother and father would be sound asleep when he got in. But, these days, his father might be asleep in a chair, head flopped back, mouth open, glass with a ring of milk at the bottom on the floor along with a white rum bottle by his feet. His mother would be stationed near the front door, pumping her feet, driving that sewing machine over one garment or another. He had just gone on a day trip with a whole heap of church people. He would say as much. He hoped they would have no cause to sigh and hum hymns, to talk to God about him as if he was not there.

AS AN ONLY CHILD, Auncil often wished he'd had siblings, other people who could share the job of carrying his parents' dreams. He felt like he lived on a tightrope. He had to be what his parents wanted. They deserved a good son. And he had to have his life. It was his! When he was about twelve years old, he would climb the highest tree in the backyard, the Blackie mango tree that seemed bigger than the house. He pulled and pushed himself higher and higher, ignoring the sap that stuck to his hands and feet, feeling the power of his body until he was perched mere inches from the top.

From there he sat and watched whatever he could see through the leaves: the other houses in the town, the cars, the people, the sea. Once he had stayed so long, his parents came looking for him. He heard them calling his name, shouting louder and louder. He saw then come through the back door and walk around the house shouting at the top of their lungs. "AUNCIL! AUNCIIIL!!" He could tell they were in a panic, but he did not want to give in just yet. He did not want to have to choose them over his moment above it all.

His mother marched back into the house and he watched her exit through the front and walk down the street, still shouting, her head swiveling from side to side. His father also went back in through the back door only to go out the front and search in the opposite direction as his wife. He could tell they were losing their minds. He wanted to say, "I'm here. Don't worry." But he also wanted to sit as high in a tree as he'd like and not have to answer to anyone.

Eventually, he came down and waited for them in his bedroom. His parents returned together, sweating and darkened by their screaming in the hot sun. When his father saw him, he stumbled into a chair, the relief so overpowering. His mother, however, grabbed a broom and rushed at him with a fury he had never seen. "You wan' kill me?! A weh you deh all dis time?!" He stammered the truth: he had been sitting in the big mango tree in the back.

She beat him until she cried. "I think you dead. . . . I think him dead and him a sit up in a tree a watch me!"

Auncil cowered on his bed. The places where she had struck him stung more and more with each minute. If only his life could be his own, just his own. If only he could be loved as much as he was loved by them and not be made to smother his freedom in the service of their feelings.

He watched her leave the room without looking at him. Then he heard her crying and heaving for too many minutes afterward.

SITTING IN THE TRAIN, heading back to Kingston, Auncil felt like he was on his way in every way. At 11 p.m., the heat of the day was long gone and Auncil was glad to be at a window. He watched the trees bend to the will of the wind and the force of the train. He watched the stars shine brighter in this part of Jamaica than even over his home perched on a hill in Harbour View. He would sleep well tonight, he thought. And tomorrow he would start that job with the Bank of Nova Scotia. His degree would finally get to work and give his mother the easier life she deserved. Perhaps, make enough to find his father help for his arthritis, enough help to separate him from that bottle of white rum.

But he would not give up racing. He would probably move out and get one of those new homes in the housing schemes being built all over the parish. He would have his own home, his own life, his own freedom to come and go as he pleased.

His mother would make it like he was killing them even though he would take care of them for as long as he breathed. Upset as she would be, he must live on his own. How could he really enjoy his life otherwise? How could he go on only feeling the thrill of being alive when he was hurtling down a hill, tensely perched on a bicycle?

THE FIRST RACE he participated in was by chance. He was riding his bicycle up a hill and he came across a group of cyclists lined up across the road. He pulled to the side to see what they were about and watched as they raced down the hill at full speed, a devil-may-care look on their faces. He had to join in.

Goodison

After they passed him, he turned around and let his bike barrel down the hill. He was like a bullet. As he rounded a corner, he glimpsed the sheer drop to his right, the road a mere cut in the side of a mountain. In that second, he was on top of the world, full of life like he had never been before. It was him, his body, his heart, his very life all at the mercy of his will.

He had to do it again and again, and again.

AS THE TRAIN made its way from Mo'Bay, Auncil felt the breeze increase its rush across his face and the arm he had rested on the windowsill. It was almost like he was riding down those hills again, hurtling toward that finish line and giddy from the rush of his blood.

He closed his eyes and tried to tune out the sound of the train's engine. He let the wind remind his skin. He could live like a victor. . . .

He did not know how much time passed before he heard the train's whistle blow and felt the car tilt as it traveled a curve. Auncil opened his eyes to a sky that seemed darker even as the stars were more pronounced. He squinted into the distance, hoping to see the skyline. He looked as hard as he could and waited for his eyes to adjust to the night, enough for him to see all he could as he journeyed home. He searched for that line between heaven and Earth, but he was not sure he could make it out.

TWO TRIBUTES

Terrance Hayes

LYNDA HULL (1954-1994)

Lynda Hull, like Walt Whitman, not to mention Dorothy Parker, William Carlos Williams, Allen Ginsberg, W. S. Merwin, Anne Waldman, Patti Smith, Amiri Baraka, was born on the mystifying planet of New Jersey. Hull's poems are as incendiary as the lighter fluid inside the sturdy, stainless steel Zippo lighter she stole from her father, a spout of spitfire, when she ran away from home at 16. "I remember this the way I'd remember a knife against my throat: that night, after the overdose, you told me to count, to calm myself," Hull writes in "Counting in Chinese," a poem derived, one assumes, from Hull's years high as the moon on the lamb in Chinatown, married to a gambler from Shanghai. Taking up her pen & mostly laying down her syringe, Hull was divorced & remarried to a poet by 1984, living on fugitive wonder & figurative language, lines of Hopkins & Akhmatova in Arkansas & later, Indiana. Hull sometimes read her poems wearing dangling earrings & ankle-strapped high heels with her flapper's hairdo dyed the same color as her beret. In addition to lighter fluid, Hull's poems display the properties of rain just before it evaporates. Hull's poems hold saltwater: "Tide of Voices" in *Ghost Money* (1986), "Shore Leave" in *Star Ledger* (1991); "Rivers into Seas" in *The Only World* (1995), published a year after her death in a car crash in Provincetown a few miles from the beach. When she wakes on the other side, Hull spends the hours she's not writing poetry mulling figures of wonder with holy wine while listening to fugitive jazz. Sometimes Bird appears with his horn on the cover of *Ornithology.* Having retained her uncanny ability to channel varieties of sound, Hull scats to Bird like Ella Fitzgerald wiping sweat from her brow. Sometimes ghosts come by. When she was alive, Hull memorized the entirety of "The Bridge," a fifty-six-page multi-section poem about the Brooklyn Bridge written by Hart Crane, Hull's favorite poet, in 1923 when he was twenty-three & working as a copywriter in Cleveland, nine years before his suicide. Hart Crane comes by sometimes. Hull regales him with passages of "The Bridge" long into the eternal evening.

MICHAEL S. HARPER (1938-2016)

Beneath the hat is a brain born in Brooklyn in 1938. Beneath the hat is "My Father's Face," "My Mother's Bible." Beneath the hat is Robert Hayden, the Negro Folk Tradition, Providence, the speckled blues-poet-professor-mentor Sterling Brown & the mad-sanctifying-farmer-turned-abolitionist John Brown. Beneath the hat is "The Militance of a Photograph in the Passbook of a Bantu under Detention" which opens with *"Peace is the active presence of Justice"* & details a black man with pus swaddling his bandages. Beneath the hat is the shape of an oak's trunk laid bare by the homicidal chainsaw of the State. Beneath the hat is Coltrane asleep on a train dreaming the names of trees between New York & Philly. Beneath the hat is "MSH." Beneath the hat is all of "History as Apple Tree," "History as Polka Dots & Moonbeans," "History as Diabolical Materialism." Beneath the hat is the ghost of the brother who died in a motorcycle accident. Harper had two children who died at birth. "Song: *I Want a Witness*." Beneath the hat is a church of four black girls blown up in Alabama, a net of five hundred middle passage blacks under water in Charleston harbor. Cries & songlines spill from a tenor tethered to the gut of a black man playing on a warped record playing on a warped record player beneath the hat. Beneath the hat is "American History," "Bigger's Blues," "Elvin's Blues," "Martin's Blues," a black man's view of suffering, a black man's view of beauty, a black man's view of faith. Beneath the hat is a place a black man can place a few small apples for his children. Beneath the hat is the oily salty smell clinging to the skin of the apples when the children eat them.

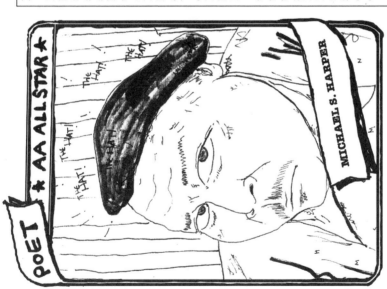

THE BAKER'S TALE
Reginald McKnight

THERE WAS THIS BOY who walked the threadbare path between his hamlet and this small, lively town at the end of the path. People called the boy Bread because he never spoke or read or played with the other boys, but stayed home with his mother and baked bread to sell at the market. They made angel bread, black bread, silver bread, devil bread, pine bread, and three-river bread. All were delicious—sweet where they were supposed to be and bitter or savory in the right places. It was always warm, even up to the third day. People, animals, and gardens—even gardens—loved it, ate it up in their roots.

The boy's job was to sell pine bread to the townspeople at the end of the threadbare path. He must do this every Friday afternoon before the threadbare path grew too dim for travel back to his hamlet. The people of that town used the bread—braided and dusted with black sesame seeds—in a ritual that went back to the beginning of days, and they needed it warm and fresh no later than one hour before sunset. Naturally, many baked their own bread, but the bread the boy and mother baked hummed like a gong. The 200 or so loaves were swept off his cart in less than half an hour. He and his old blind horse usually made it home just as the sun was setting.

But during the spring the boy turned eleven, the town was struck by a horrible vibrio, so instead of selling in the empty market, Bread walked his horse and cart up and down the streets, selling his wares like a dairyman. Though he began leaving at midday, he rarely made it halfway home before nightfall, and so he would have to pick his way down the threadbare path like a blind dog, on all fours, sniffing, feeling. He took to leaving home, therefore, in the early morning, rising from his mother's bed before his eyes were open, and making his blind way with the blind horse; he would be mid-trail when the air was pale scarlet. He grew to adore this hour. Spring was coming earlier than usual and the negro-tongue blossoms were up, beaded with dew and sap. Red-throats hovered amid them, feeding, flirting. The lilac lilies were poised to open, their lips gently parted, their sweet breath already in the air. Bread's blood flushed to the surface of his skin at this hour. His lungs and heart grew radiant. The old horse's ears flicked toward every sound, her canter youthful, supple. She was pink in tongue and lip.

Every such morning was good, but only insofar as the threadbare path was concerned. The arrival always shocked him. The vibrio made the people stagger through the streets, and bleed from their ears, and speckle like rotting leaves, and cramp and twist and rattle and die. It was bitter to his eyes. The vibrio ate up the people for its every meal, but they went about, even in their grieving, as calm as snuff boxes.

One Friday afternoon, he asked a smithy if his faith gave him courage before his afflictions. The smithy handed over the money for the two loaves, spat pink on his own boot, and said, "What's one to do with the other?"

Each morning on the threadbare path, spring burgeoned, and every morning Bread would see and the horse would hear and smell new flowers, new beasts, emerging from hibernation. There would be new spider webs, both violet and white. A giant horn wing might buzz his ears to show him who is king, or a small pink butterfly might ride the horse's haunch for three full miles. One Friday he saw a giant green roach and a golden roach scuttling under the same rock for fear of the horse's hooves. The next Friday he thought he saw the great green one eating the hind parts of his golden former compatriot. He also saw three Chester's lizards sunning themselves, three blue ribbons on a carpet of moss, not a horse-length away. One of them watched the roach from the joint of his eye, and that eye did not once break its gaze. "It's all eating in this forest," Bread mumbled to the horse.

But one late spring day, three toads started from his footfall—in the sloppy way they leap, of course. Even the small ones land like sacks of pudding and, in order to take a subsequent leap, must gather their limbs together like so many yarrow stalks under their pudding bodies. They are easy to catch, though few animals touch them. Bread slowed his pace to let them pass into the elbow grass, which grows thick all along the threadbare path. Not long thereafter, 2 more toads pitched themselves away from the horse and boy, and vanished again into the elbow grass, and 2 more stood in profile on a stone the size of a man's head, and 4 more stared at him from a low banyan branch, and 30 clung to the tree's massive trunk, and 12 of them were on the opposite side of the path, on a stone the size of a man's trunk, and over 40 watched as they sat on a mat of rusty needles under an ancient vinegar pine. And over 300 of them bobbed up and down and over and across one another's backs and upturned bellies as they moved to clear themselves from the threadbare path. Then, the path took the usual sharp curve around an enormous boulder, and when boy and horse completed the near circuit, the toads were an uncountable mass. The Earth's skin, it seemed to Bread, had become a million toads. So heavy they were, that they pressed the elbow grass clean to the soil. The horse, the boy, could not move.

Bread's mother told him one morning as she bathed him, "Don't kill what you don't eat: lobster flowers, cinnamon birds, tassels, Chester's, and toads. All those creatures, all of 'em, or anything like 'em, are full of poison. Each in its own way'll wart you up, or shrink your manhood, or kill the baby inside the woman, or make you see life as it's not, or make you clear on things that are a burden to know. Hear me good and tight, boy. You see these things you tip your cap and say, 'By your leave, madam or sir,' and go on about selling our loaves."

So, the whole world, for a spell, seemed bitter with toads, and the boy did not lead the horse, and the horse did not so much as flick an ear, even though, by and by, the toads began to chirr, as they do at nightfall, and the mass was so shrill and loud, it tore the air into specks. Bread began to weep, and he pressed his wrists into his ears, and the horse knelt in fear, so Bread unlatched her from the cart, and when he did, she lay down completely. The broken air was full of the toads' sound, the smell of them filled the places where the quiet had gone, and his every atom revulsed, and he vomited hard and sharp at his feet.

Bread saw through his tears that the creatures were still at the work of clearing themselves off the threadbare path. There always come those times when forward is identical to backward, so Bread patted the trembling horse on her rump, secured her harness, and urged her up the hill. They moved ever so slowly, through the shattered air, as the path resolved, and up they went until they reached the crest of the hill. There, Bread saw what at first he thought was a bearhound, but as he moved closer he understood that he beheld an enormous toad. Its huge back was turned toward Bread, but the boy knew the great thing could see him and the old horse just as well as he could see the toad. A toad, his mother told him, can see you coming and going.

Bread forced his jittering frame closer, and the toad turned three-quarters round to face him, gazed at him from head to toe. All Bread could manage was to return the gaze. The great toad was black, mostly, but had a yellowish belly, freckled here and there with brown. Its eyes rose mechanically—tick, tick, tick—reptilian, not smooth like the mammal. He began at Bread's feet, and his eye scanned him from his ankles up. At the very moment they met eye to eye, the hill, the path, the grasses, the bushes, the treetops fell into quiet. Not only were the million toads silent, but the whole world felt devoid of sound, and when it was at its most silent, a silence so heavy he could not hear his own thoughts, Bread knew he would enter the town, and he knew what he would find. The great toad turned its back again in order to face the town, and took several long leaps toward the small copse of trees, the place where the threadbare path ends and the town road begins. Boy and horse followed toad. The great silence followed horse, toad, and boy. The great toad would not

McKnight

enter the town, but horse and boy, they went on in. Bread knew this would happen, and what they were supposed to do. They went on in.

No beast or being, two-legged or four-, traversed the street; no fires burned at roadside stands; no ladies selling feather hats or wicker boxes; no butchers; no taxis; no postal women or brickmen or porters or constables. No clergy in their pointed shoes and long beards. No clotillo players with their sheet music and upturned hats. No academy girls in their green frocks and flat caps; no turnbulls in starchy white uniforms; no leggers with the wide leather belts; no trench horses, muddy from hoof to fetlock to knee to belly. No mendicants, dockmen, cantor boys, regulators, dairymaids, stevedores—no guide, guard, or hen dogs. No partridges, doves, sparrows, cinnamons, spires, hawks, or ducks in the pond, or chickens in pens. No cats. No mice. Not a one.

The air, grey with flies, smelled of mildew and the sweet horror that lies three days beyond putrefaction, and Bread knew he must be thorough, and go from home to home, building to building—not, of course, to sell his pine bread, but to feed what was left of the town. So, he must have entered 500 homes, 81 shops, 3 temples, 9 civic buildings, the Great Park, the 3 market streets with their dozens of kiosks. He opened each kiosk. He found no one, alive or dead. Everything was cloaked in grey. Even the air was dead. The silence followed him like a pet dog. He led the horse back to the center of town and sat by the well in the Great Park. He ate his food, and fed and watered the horse. He gave her hay and pine bread, and she ate trumpet and elbow grasses on her own.

As the boy ate his meat and rested, the old horse's ears pricked to something only she could hear. He turned in the direction her ears were cupped and saw a small lad in a green kaftan and yellow slippers, sitting on a banyan branch, not eighty paces from where he was sitting. It was some time after sunset, but still light enough to see this bird-necked child with the bird-bright eyes. Bread realized he must have walked right by the boy at least twice on his search for survivors. Or perhaps the boy had been following him the whole time, but how could a boy so young and raised in a town be so cagey? Whatever the case, the boy did not seem afraid as Bread walked toward him, but remained silent, looking relieved to see another living face. He did not smile, but looked hopeful, expectant and appallingly weary. Before Bread was quite twenty paces from the foundling, he said, "Are you alone?"

"Alone?" said the boy.

"Yes, 'alone'. Are you alone?"

"You alone," said the boy.

Only ten paces from the boy, Bread halted, raised his hands, palms upward. He said, "Just me and my friend over there—the horse."

"The horse," said the boy.

"Where are your parents, little boy?"

"Your parents, little boy?"

Bread began to understand, so experimentally, he said, "Dragonfly."

"Dragonfly," said the boy.

"Lilac lily, golden cup, club-leaf tea."

"Golden cup, club tea."

So he understood: the boy could speak, could even pronounce words better than a child his age usually does, but he doubted there would be much understanding between them. Bread closed the small gap between himself and the boy. He smiled, nodded, hoping to reassure, and lifted the boy off the branch. "Light as a feather," he muttered.

McKnight

"A feather," the boy said.

"You're all alone in the world. I'll take you home."

"Take you home."

"I don't think you're feeble-minded, though."

"Minded, though."

Bread carried the boy to his cart, and offered the boy meat. The boy refused it, but he ate lots of bread, and drank four cups of tea. He could not tell Bread what became of the people of the town, and Bread realized the boy might not even truly understand, and perhaps by the time he was old enough to understand, he would have no memory of what he had seen.

Bread built a fire as the grey sky grew black, and as the fire roared and cracked, he lifted the boy into the cart and laid him atop the warm loaves. He covered the boy with the horse blanket, but abruptly the boy sat up and his black bird eyes grew wide in the light of the fire. He clutched the horse blanket in his bird-claw hands and whispered, "Will happen to me! Happen to me!" Bread felt his heart thump hard four or five times, and for a moment he couldn't hear the fire, or the snoring horse, but his own blood beating the sides of his head. He had been stunned not only by the boy's sudden uproar, but this new wrinkle in his being. And he climbed up in his cart and wrapped an arm around the boy's bony shoulders. The embrace brought him as much comfort as it might have given the lad. And then, words rose up to him from the very earth, words that he did not think of before he spoke them.

He said, "The people of your town, and all the horses, dogs, birds, show monkeys, chimeras, fish, worms, mice, all of it, everyone, it looks like, took to fever and it's made toads of 'em all. Even the chancel-mayor took sick and toaded up. It was a merciless thing, but there's good in it, since they're still alive." He paused, touched his fingertips to his chin as though in thought, but he wasn't thinking at all. "So much alive they'll never be eaten by anything, and they'll never rot up even if they do die. You catch my way, boy? They won't live forever, but they'll live good lives free of jobs and religions, and they'll sleep all winter under rocks and soft brown leaves. And each toad is all the way clannish, and all the way free. They don't go to war, and they look after their own in their own way. You don't have to worry about your family bush whatsoever again. They'll eat and carry on. They had me come here and look for you.

"What you and me'll do next, see, we'll chummy on back to my hamlet, and we'll see what we see. I'm just about the solest one who comes up this way, and it's all sick here, now see. . . ." Bread paused to let his mouth fill up again from where these words were coming. He said, "They'll run us off, you and me. We'll knock on door after door, but not one will open to let us in. Not even my own mother. They'll run us off, and that'll be OK because I'm your brother, and you are mine. I think we're probably half toad, anyway, you and me, and we might will live pretty close to forever. I'll teach you to bake bread, and we'll find you a name, and I'll teach you to chalk up and feed a carthorse, and like I say, we just might will live pretty close to forever. Even this good horse. She's likely half toad, too, seeing as they sent both of us to find you."

Bread felt golden in his lungs, and his knees trembled. He lifted his arm from the boy's shoulder and climbed down from the cart and made a bed for himself next to the fire.

In the morning they rose, and away they went into the future he had spoken into being.

RUPTURES
& TRANS-
FORMATIONS

NO MORE SORROW SONGS

Metta Sáma

WHEN GALAI OPENED HER EYES that autumn morning, she found herself looking directly into the utter blackness at the edges of Earth. The whites of her mother's eyes were so clear, the black looked stultifying, like a murder of crows attempting to blot out a cloud. The red ring around the black was merely imagined, she was sure of it, a foreboding sign that she had come to associate with her mother. She leaned back into her pillow, hoping to sink into nothingness, to fall, haphazardly, into a private space that her dead brother and father occupied, but the sound of Ommi's breath, a hiss that sounded more steaming radiator than human, pulled her out of herself.

"Get on up now, Galai," Ommi said and quickly stood, as if she'd been talking to herself, walking over to the light switch to wave it on. The room was suddenly an eruption of yellow—butterscotch light dripping from the ceiling, heavy medallion yellow of the curtains, scrubbed canary, bumblebee, daffodil, dandelion yellows of the quilt, her mother's voice, too, burnt honey yellow. Colors to brighten the mood of the room, Ommi had said, in one of her rare attempts to sweep up sorrow and burn it in the garden. The sound of crisp dead leaves shaking free from the pin oaks penetrated the room.

Her mother's body heavily landed on the bed again, a physics equation that Galai couldn't work out. Ommi was desperately thin; were it not for her weighty baritone voice, she was certain her mother could be whisked away by a strong wind. A pleasurable, greedy thought she'd had since her brother's death. But without Ommi, who was she? Instinctively, she placed her hand on her stomach. Her mother's eyes moved away from the misery in her child's body.

"We gone be late if you don't get up now." Ommi rose from the bed, made her way to the curtains and began to gently squeeze and twist them, a sign that the pain had caught her again. "I know you don't want to do this, Galai, but you got to, you got no choice in the matter."

"And what about you, Ommi? What about you?" Galai knew the risk of talking back to this mother, the one so engulfed in pain that she was quick to snap, quick to release her agony on anyone near her.

As if to prove her strength, Ommi straightened her body, her hand an iron, pressing the fabric straight, before yanking the curtains open, letting the early morning darkness in. She smiled at her child, still lying in bed, and began to hum a morning song she used to sing to all three of her children, back when they were all hers, before their household turned into a household much like the other households in Mina, North Carolina, places of suffering and then of lifelong grief cloaked under the righteousness of God. Galai always wanted to ask her mom: *If god is so good, like all of the time, why he let so many of us bear so much pain? What we do to this world to be treated like this?* But she knew her mother would say what they all said, that God was testing their strength, that Heaven waited on the other side. She raised her voice to ask again, "What about you?" but before the sound escaped, a terrible pain took hold of her mother, who whirled around, grabbed hold of the window ledge, and rested her forehead on the cool pane.

WHEN GALAI'S BROTHER was still alive, the three of them—Fadia, Galai, and Hosiah—would trace the waves of their mother's sometimes breezy, sometimes booming, holy singing voice. Other than the occasional children's song, Ommi only sang the old-time gospel that could be heard any Sunday, Wednesday, or Friday at the First Baptist Pentecostal Church at Mina. The children preferred secular music, the upbeat music of their generation, music that captured the swells of rebellion, desire, friendship, mischief, and debauchery. But they dutifully sang

> *We are soldiers in the army*
> *We have to fight although we have to cry*
> *We have to hold up the blood-stained banner*
> *We got to hold it until we die*

even though none of them wanted to die in an army battle, not even the quick-to-temper Fadia who, by age eight, had developed

Sáma

a reputation as a burgeoning bully. They sang to feel the thread between child and mother strengthen; they sang to feel the freedom that their mother sang about when she sang the song of sparrows. Fadia, being the oldest, would try to match her mother note for note, would challenge Ommi's authority by daring to battle her in song. Ommi seemed to relish those moments, testing her vocal strength, switching between octaves to see if her child had the makings to be the youngest lead singer in the church choir.

The evening of their father's death, Fadia, angered by her grief, no words to explore the feeling of one day having a dad toss your twelve-year-old frame into the air, and the next day hearing through the neighborhood gossip line that your dad wouldn't be throwing anyone into the air anymore, wouldn't even be returning home anymore, that kind of languageless anguish, sparked a fire that Fadia had been working to dampen. So, when Ommi raised her voice in ululation, sounding the mourning bell, Fadia did the unthinkable, raised her voice against Ommi's, rendered her mother's loss and pain as nothing compared to the loss and pain of Fadia. Mother's grief versus daughter's grief. It was the first crack in their foundation, a loving foundation that had been so strong it flowed into the streets, brought neighbors and strangers to their stairs, lingering, wanting in on that family love. Fadia would say the crack wasn't her fault, but the fault of the foreman for causing such tremendous dread to enter their household, was her mother's for not barreling into the factory and pushing the foreman over the rail that took her father's life, was her father's for not paying attention to where he was going, was God's, for being a cruel and meaningless god.

OMMI'S BREATHING SLOWED, but she kept her head pressed against the pane. Galai dug deeper into her bed, imagined the quilt was her cocoon, a place to shield her eyes from the sight of a dying mother. Her longing for not-ill Ommi increased with every family loss and that longing had begun to make her feel fractured. One part of her wanted to cut Ommi down, another part of her wanted to pick her mother up, plant her somewhere safe, somewhere the soil was rich and not drenched in chemicals, give her mother a second chance at strength.

As if Galai's thoughts had reached her, Ommi grabbed hold of the window crank and rolled her wrist, an action that Galai knew must be painful. The autumn chill eased into the room, bringing with it a sense, Galai thought, of renewal. She willed her mother to turn around, to meet her eyes, to see the apology there, to see the love there, but she still couldn't open her mouth to speak that longing, to speak that love. How could she look at that body, that dying body, and not hate it for its fear, for its trust that God would provide?

"Come on, now, Galai, I'm not gonna tell you again. This ain't no time to be acting like a scared little baby."

Galai's eyes glinted. Her mother, too afraid to do for her body what she was allowing for Galai's body, enraged the young child. Every day, she watched Ommi's body heave from the pain, listened to the sound of the fork clinking against the plate, her mother's hand holding up her head, looking all the world like a toddler bored by mealtimes. And yet, here she was, fear draining the life from her eyes, telling her child to be brave.

Sáma

Galai knew her mother feared doctors, and with good reason. They'd seen more than one young Black woman driven to the hospital by a celebratory husband only for the husband to return, defeated, with a baby and no wife. Her own grandmother had had so much of her body cut away that by the time Galai was old enough to sit on her lap, all that was left of her was a torso with truncated limbs. Their father had told them all about the doctors experimenting on Black women's bodies, had shown them the medieval tools the doctors' used, the refusal of anesthesia. Had told them about the Black pilots, the young mother who went to the doctor time and again only to be told she was imagining things, that same young mother whose body was still in the hospital, cells spliced over and over. Their mother told them about the eugenics program that gave doctors permission to sterilize single mothers if they had more than two babies and were on government assistance.

"All a y'all lucky to even be here," Ommi would tell the children. "Shiiiiiii with all them doctors neutralizing the women round here, taking away their rights without their consent, it's a miracle any of these women had more than one baby."

Despite her mother's justified fear of doctors and her persistent dreams of dying under the knife, Galai still couldn't muster enough love to be kind to her these past years. She wanted to yell at Ommi, to throttle her, wanted to drag her to the hospital, have her own illness diagnosed, treated, wanted Ommi to become the model patient. Instead, her mother expected her, Galai, a child, to become the test for the town, to be wheeled into the great unknown, to lie in a state of suspension while masked people cut into her, removing parts of her body and, hopefully, stitching her back up without leaving behind unwanted things, scissors or gloves, clamps or tubes.

Enraged, she yanked the quilt away, tossed her legs over the mattress, and casually shouldered Ommi out of her path, knowing her mother's weight wouldn't be able to withstand the attack.

LONG BEFORE the Sanctified Sisters prayed over the bulge in Galai's abdomen, long before her brother's and father's apparitions began visiting her, reminding her that she had an important role to fulfill, she knew she had a part to play in this small town, a big part that would depend on giving her body over to a power greater than a religious god. She knew, intuitively, that the townspeople would look to her to provide a path. The Miracle Child, they'd call her. The One Who Made It Out. And although the Sanctified Sisters said there was no power greater than God, they'd taken a special interest in her after Hosiah's death. Had shadowed her, cornered her to form prayer circles around her. Her body would be the key to their truer salvation, a belief in science. But how that would happen, Galai couldn't figure out. Their loyalty to God displaced all other beliefs. When their kin died, slowly, horribly, the way Hosiah had, they said the devil had got hold of them, had promised them a better life in exchange for faithfulness. They betrayed God, and God took away his mercy. It was all God, they'd said. God had a plan for them.

Sáma

ALONE, Galai stood at her window, watching the leaves slip from their branches, curl and dance. A long, slow wind blew; the fallen leaves gathered strength, lifted from the ground, swirled, dropping and rising, struggling. She willed the leaves to take the shape of Hosiah, hair still thick and picked straight out, body still thin in the freshly laundered pajamas he was wearing when he left this world two years ago, at eleven years old. Lately, he struggled to appear, wavering as his voice warbled. She knew he was moving closer and closer to some new place, some irresistible place, a place akin to but not Ommi's Heaven, in which neither of them believed. When the leaves settled back onto the ground, Galai cursed her sister and the other Sanctifieds, who, she'd decided, were bullying the town's otherworld with their constant loud praying, making the spirits either reluctant to visit or too weak. The leaves, curved and lifeless on the ground, set her mind on her body. What would it be when it was freed from this torment?

She recalled playing in the woods with her siblings and parents, a game called Previous and Future Forms that her father loved.

"What were you before you were you? What will you be next?"

They discovered the answers in the woods: if an object chose them, it was their past self; if they chose the object, it was their future self.

"The path to the future lies in accepting the past and understanding the past," their father would tell them. "Only nonbelievers in the power of the Earth would be foolish enough to rush towards an uncertain future."

But Fadia and her mother, both impetuous people, would rush into the woods, seeking the most beautiful or elusive or difficult-to-capture object. Galai, Hosiah, and their father preferred to let the object find them, to take their time and enjoy listening to and breathing in the trees and soil and flowers.

One day, her brother, lying in the woods next to their father, asked: "Why were there only seven days in Ommi's Bible stories? What would have happened on the eighth day?" Their father sat up so quickly the twins thought he was angry, but the look on his face was reverence.

"Perhaps on the eighth day, a god would have made actual children instead of the adult children of your Ommi's Bible."

"And why would God do that?"

"Perhaps to take the time to understand the nature of human behavior, the true nature that comes with growing up, growing beyond the will of your parent."

"But isn't that what happened already, to Eve?"

"Yes, but Eve came into the world as an adult already. She had no real time to grow, to learn, to listen. And God, God had no time to grow, to learn, to listen, to truly understand humans."

"Are you saying God is flawed?"

"I'm saying Ommi's Bible doesn't always have the right answers."

Hosiah and Galai had sat there, looking at their father look at them, so much trust in his eyes, so much love. These private moments with their father made them feel full, whole, precious.

GALAI COULD HEAR her mother in the kitchen, preparing food to last her through the long hours of Galai's surgery. She looked beyond her yard, out until she couldn't see anymore, out to the main path to the river she used to love. The plant was far enough up the road that its buildings were hidden by lush trees, but the smoke pumping up and out looked like clouds to the children.

A century ago, some women had got it into their heads to populate the forest of Mina with fragrant flower seeds, sweet smelling herbs, flowering vines and sweet grasses, some transplanted redwoods they knew would one day grow to be taller than the factory, groves of fruit trees and surprise patches of wild alliums. All to disguise the noxious gases pluming in the cloud-smoke.

By the time Galai and her siblings came into the world, the woods were a dizzying experience, wild and cultivated. Butterflies and strange bees, dragonflies and clearwing sphinx moths, a lake the residents had dug out of the river's course so everyone could eat safe fish and the kids could have a place to swim, but which now also collected the plant's runoff. Rumor had it that the city council of the affluent neighboring town of Maynard had voted to put warning signs in the river, near their running trail, saying that partaking of too much of the river and lake could lead to poisoning. But no such signs populated the shores of Mina.

The mayor insisted residents were fabricating. "Aren't the waters abundant with food?" he asked at a press conference. "And aren't you all the ones constantly boasting of the majesty of your woods?" Despite the mayor's public dismissal of their concern, a small group of citizens continued to protest.

Galai left her bedroom, waded through the spiritual that her mother was now releasing into the air, her mother's voice strong again, infused with the word of God. In the bathroom, she grabbed hold of one of the bottles of water that her mother now left on the bathroom counter for face washing and teeth brushing, a silent sign that she now believed what the town activists had been saying about the water, about the plant.

Yet despite the numerous illnesses plaguing the community, the minister still refused to acknowledge that the plant was killing their water, that the water was killing them. Galai thought back to the last sermon she went to, soon after her twelfth birthday, a year after her brother had died. God, the minister was once again sermonizing, created this land of ours on the eighth day, a day erased from the Bible, but dwelling within us, a secret too sacred to be written. The forest was abundant. No one went hungry, he'd said, again. If anyone was to blame for the ailments plaguing the community, it was the community members themselves, living their sin-filled lives.

"GOD!" the minister had shouted, "GOD! Our mighty GOD who lets us not call him by his given name, but by his ACTION, the ACTION of GOD: GOODNESS OVER DAMNATION, GOD! has put us here, brethren, sistren, GOD has put us here, in this place, this almighty beautiful place, this place that is so beautiful, ooooooooooooooooo weeeeeeeeeeeeeeeeeeeee when men see it, they drop to they knees and promise allegiance to it, they beg to be taken in, they promise to take care of this place to nurture it to honor it to build upon it they treat it, brethren you know you do, they treat this place like it's they woman!"

The church shouted their hallelujahs.

"But brethren brethren brethren, this place ain't no woman. This is a HOLY place a SACRED place a GOD place. God gave us this place and what we do with it? Huh? I say what we do with it?"

Sáma

The church shouted their lines.

"That's right, sistren, brethren, we treat it like it some woman. Some woman in a skin-tight dress and flashy red lips. Some woman with her breasts sitting nice and tall and her hair pressed and gracefully caressing her buttocks. Oh yeah, brethren, oh yeah."

The brethren murmured their desire. The sistren sucked their teeth.

"Oh brethren, this place, I say THIS HERE place this ain't your woman. You make your pretty promises to your woman and then what you do? Huh? You go on over to Rusty's Bar or Genevive's, you drink up your money, get you another woman, you pollute your body and pollute your new woman's body then go home and pollute your steady's body right after. Oh yeah I know you. I SEE you. GOD SEES YOU. Polluters. Desecraters of this Earth. THIS LAND that GOD gave us. You DESTROYERS of your bodies! You can't take care of you own woman and you prostrate to this land like she some woman you can FORGET to CARE for! Oh God SEES you. And God got an answer for you. Oh yes he does. Oh yes he does. Hallelujah! Can I get an Amen?!"

GALAI AND HER MOTHER stepped into the dim chilly morning light. Across the way they could see her sister's whites, a crescent moon peeking from behind the trees. Their mother lifted her arm, as if she were going to wave for Fadia to join them, but her arm dropped just as quickly, as if stung by the memory of Fadia denouncing her name, her family, her place as eldest sibling. Ommi lifted her chin instead, drew in a breath, exhaled, and sailed a song across the yard, across the road, into the edge of the woods, luring her sister from behind the tree, deep into the wave of air that was her mother's song.

Galai looked over at the pile of leaves outside her bedroom window which was now twirling in the air, a dance she imagined was meant to lift her spirits, ready her for the doctor. The cancers that plagued Mina were treatable, the doctor had said, if treated early, aggressively. Galai was ready for her body to be free, not only of this cancer, but of the sorrows devastating their town. She would go to the hospital, let them put her under, one step toward more pain, but also toward a kind of freedom.

DOG TIGER HORSE

Yeoh Jo-Ann

(Winner of the 2020 Aura Estrada Short Story Contest)

EDITOR'S NOTE:

Yeoh Jo-Ann sweeps us into the things that we will remember on sleepless nights, the what ifs of our lives, the way that humans break each other, those things left unsaid, and the secrets we carry. This is the kind of story that clutches at your throat and makes your heart race because you know a human collision is afoot. Yeoh targets the heart and never wavers.

—Ivelisse Rodriguez, 2020 Aura Estrada Short Story Contest judge

Tiger

The window is open.

You are under the bed, screaming. Outside, the wind whips through the trees and the rain smashes down on the roof. Lightning. Thunder. I close the window, but you cry on.

The next morning, you apologize. You are fifteen and you are embarrassed.

I don't understand, Mama. What's wrong with me?

I have watched you grow up with a fear of thunderstorms. I keep silent, but I buy us a cake to share after dinner. A small one with coconut, the kind you like.

What's the occasion? Your sister is always suspicious when she sees cake at the table. She likes cake, but she knows it is your favorite and not hers. *What are you making up for, Mama?*

Your sister is a clever girl, far cleverer than you will ever be. But she smiles to show me that she's joking, and I allow it.

For marrying you to Ah Tu, I tell her. Ah Tu is the boy who comes in twice a week to scrub the floors and clean the garden. Your sister shrieks and laughs, and I feel a flutter of guilt. But she has forgotten her question, and everyone must look down on someone. It gives us hope.

I know why you are afraid of thunderstorms, but I will not explain. I would rather take coins from my box and buy you cake.

~

When the engineer asks your father if he can marry your sister, even your grandmother is proud. She pats your sister on the cheek, saying how good it is to have a clever girl in the house, forgetting that two years ago she refused to continue paying the clever girl's school fees and that the clever girl gave up her place at the teaching college to work at a bookstore. Your sister has not forgotten. But she smiles and says thank you, so pleased with her engagement that for a moment she forgets her vow to spit into your grandmother's face on the day she leaves the house.

It is a good thing that your sister kept her temper. Even the cleverest girls cannot spin spit into money, and we cannot pay for the wedding without your grandmother's help.

It is your fault for having a daughter.

Yeoh

In her sitting room in the front of the house, your grandmother does not offer me tea, or even water. She knows I am here to beg.

You tiger women. So stubborn. She has said this to me more times than I can count, but she knows I have to listen. *Should have given the child away, like I told you to. What use is a girl?*

In the end, I give her what she wants. I kneel down in front of her and bow, lower and lower, until my forehead touches the cold marble floor. I weep. I beg.

Your father is waiting for me when I return to our room. Too much of a coward to ask his mother himself. *Did she say yes?*

I tell him there is enough for a small wedding. The next day, I sell my mother's jewelry. Except a small ring: I am saving that for your wife.

But first I must buy happiness for my clever girl.

I could have been a clever girl myself. When the first of the Japanese bombs fell on Penang, my father stopped us from going to school. And when the war was over, there was no question of going back. So I married your father and came to live in this house.

The house was tired long before I arrived. Peeling paint, all the best furniture sold. No servants left. Your grandfather's stores were closed during the war; the Japanese took everything except the stores themselves. In more prosperous times, your grandparents would have picked a better bride for your father. But they wanted a girl whose family they could sneer at, a girl your father would not feel inferior to, someone who would do the housework.

When the matchmaker first spoke to my parents, they decided it would be my eldest sister, your First Aunt, who married your father. But she was born in the year of the rat and your father in the year of the horse. Your grandmother put her foot down. *Everyone knows rats and horses make terrible matches.*

I am a tiger. A tiger and a horse—a strong match. Tigers, horses, and dogs are allies bound by the stars and the elements. They understand each other; they are stronger together. That is what the fortune-tellers say. If you ask me, it is all nonsense.

But you are not asking me. You are a child but you must already know from watching us that good marriages have nothing to do with astrology.

But good weddings start with a good dress, and that is what your sister must have. While she is at work, we will go to the fabric store in town to buy the best silk I can afford with the money from selling the jewelry. Your grandmother and aunts give us the usual incurious arched looks on our way out as we walk through the dark central corridor of the house and past your grandmother's sitting room. They sit around her marble mahjong table, drinking tea and munching on dried lotus seeds.

Going out? Nothing better to do? Your Sar Kor, your father's youngest sister, is my least favorite member of this nest of vipers. *You've ironed my dress for tomorrow?*

Have you cleaned my room? I dropped my powder case yesterday. Your Tua Kor, your eldest aunt, would not recognize a broom or dustpan if we showed these to her.

For dinner, I am thinking of fish. Ah Tu will fetch one. What your grandmother means is that I'd better be home in time to cook it.

I assure everyone that their rooms have been cleaned, their clothes ironed, that I will be back at five to begin cooking dinner.

Yeoh

Two hours is not much time to get to town and back and buy everything we need, but we must try. And if we are a little late, your grandmother's fish can wait. It has nowhere else to be.

~

Men are like that. You are a woman—adapt.

My mother refuses to hear any more stories. *You are a newly married woman. In time, you will understand. You will learn.* This is not reassurance. She is only telling me the end of my story.

Maybe things will be better when there are children.

When your sister is born, I wait for your father to become the kind of man who wants to be at home, who works hard. To stop the drinking, the gambling, the late nights.

When you are born, I wait for him to realize we are our own family now, that we need to move out of this house and into a home of our own. I wait for him to want to be a better man, a good example for his son.

That you are born in the year of the dog delights your grandmother. She leans over your cradle when you are a month old, when she is convinced you will live. *Dog—you complete the trinity, you will bring your father the horse and your mother the tiger closer, and you will be stronger together.*

But you and your sister are only children. And, as my mother keeps telling me, he is only a man.

~

The sewing machine is the only thing I own when I first arrive at this house, along with the ten bolts of cloth that are my brother's wedding gift to me, some of my mother's jewelry, and the clothes on my back.

The women of the house take the cloth. *You won't have anywhere to wear silks to.*

They let me keep the sewing machine. *Let her make her own clothes. As it is, she's already an extra mouth to feed.*

And the jewelry. *Quite poor quality.*

On my trips to the market, I stop by the old tailor's and collect cut-up fabric that I put together into dresses in the evenings after dinner. In time, I make more complicated clothes, in cuts I will never wear myself. I learn to make leg-of-mutton sleeves, a sheath dress; I master the three-inch cheongsam collar.

I put all the money the tailor pays me in a small wooden box. Most months, I take most of it out again. Your father's allowance will not stretch to cover his evening entertainments and all the things a growing family needs—books, shoes, socks, underwear, bus fare. Your grandmother pays the school fees and complains about it every month.

I ask the tailor for more work.

~

When my eldest sister, your First Aunt, first tells me about your father's other entertainments, I realize how little holds my world together. You are only seven, your sister has just turned fourteen, and your father is hopeless.

Do you know where your husband was last night?

That mahjong place. As always.

Wrong. My friend saw him go into a hotel.

I shake my head. *He works at a hotel.*

My sister takes my hand and sighs. *Not that one. Another one. On Love Lane.*

Your father is exactly the kind of man careless enough and foolish enough to conduct an affair on Love Lane, where all the rich businessmen keep their mistresses. He probably thinks this somehow makes it acceptable, being in the territory of other philanderers.

Swee was with him.

Swee. Your father's best friend since boyhood. Of course. Another rich, honey-tongued boy. Of course they decided together that taking mistresses was a thing that all men did.

When I leave your First Aunt's house, before I head home to cook the family dinner, I go to the tailor and ask him for more work.

~

It takes years, but living in this house has taught me patience. The waiting is easy. While I squat in the back garden, sweating, scrubbing the family's laundry under the trickle of the tap no one wants to repair, I think of the places I will go. While I pluck chickens clean in the dark, damp kitchen, I dream of windows in a room of my own. While you and your sister sleep, I sew and sew and sew.

When there is enough money in my box, I leave. I decide that the gods and my children will forgive me. I take my sewing machine and my mother's jewelry and the clothes on my back.

~

I cannot sleep. Outside, the rain is crashing down on the roof.

Your husband is here.

I go to my sister's front door and look out. Your father is at the gate, holding an umbrella. You are with him. Lightning lights up the street and your faces. Now thunder follows, like a monster released into the sky. You are frightened. You cling to the bars of the gate and shake them, you cry out again and again. I cannot hear you but I cannot bear not to.

I see the end of my story now. I go to my sister and tell her I am going home.

The next day, she sends my sewing machine back to the old house.

I am using it now to finish your sister's wedding dress. She will look like a queen, and I hope he will treat her like one.

Horse

Everyone knows my uncle gave me the job at the hotel because my father didn't want me in his stores, and my mother didn't want me at home. *The elder son cannot stay home. Makes the family look bad.*

Every day I go to the hotel and pretend to be important. I sit in my office. I walk around and check on the staff. I count the cash in the safe. I do as much work in the garden as I can without making the gardener uncomfortable. I try to be useful. Last week, I changed a light bulb in the third-floor corridor.

The hotel is not what it was. That's what my father says, but it's hard to imagine it being any different. At the best of times, half the rooms are occupied. This week, we have only five guests. But I like it better here than at any of the stores, where everyone talks loudly and at the same time and no one ever listens.

No one ever listens to me. Not my mother. Not the children. Not you. But I don't mind. I sit in the garden and I smoke. I tend to my plants. I know I'm not a clever man. And I know talking doesn't make me any cleverer.

Yeoh

As I watch you work on our daughter's wedding dress every evening, I am reminded that I married a clever woman. How skillful you are! The engineer too will be marrying a clever woman: Is he ready for this? I wanted to ask him three weeks ago when he came to see me at my office, bowing respectfully, waiting to be asked to sit down, choosing the old, straight-backed, uncomfortable chair instead of the newer, softer one. But we talked of other things—his job at the new chemical plant in Bayan Lepas, the house he is planning to buy.

I will take care of her. He didn't smile. To be perfectly honest, I think the fellow is a bit too serious.

Marriage is a complicated thing. I tried to sound wise; I now have the grey hair for it.

I will work very hard. I will work like a horse.

It was the thing about the horse that got me. It made me want to reach out and take his hand. It made me want to tell him everything about us, the difficulty of us. But I didn't. I nodded and said nothing and gave the man permission to marry our daughter, if she would have him.

Horses are unimaginative, the fortune-teller told my father when I was a boy. Horses can be stubborn. Impulsive. But they are loyal and hard-working. *You see your boy's ears, the way they stick out a little at the top? He will be vain and bad with money.* My father was not pleased, and the fortune-teller didn't leave the house with quite as many gifts as she could have gotten. After she left, he stared at me, at my ears. I think he started to see the business he'd built turning to dust in my hands, his fortune passing through my incapable fingers like sand. He tried but he couldn't unsee it.

Just as well, just as well. I'm not a clever man. I know that. It's fine.

In Madam Lim's mahjong parlor, I don't have to be clever. I play a few games, drink a bit of brandy, smoke a few French cigarettes. I don't have to be anyone. You don't like it when I go out in the evenings—long ago, you dismissed it as rich-boy recklessness. Is it? I don't feel very reckless.

~

The dress looks nice.

You look up from the sewing machine and smile, pleased at the compliment. But then you frown from habit. *What do you know about dresses?*

This could have come out playfully, but it doesn't. I think perhaps you want it to, but then the words sharpen themselves as they push through your head and heart and throat, and they come out pointed.

I turn away. *Nothing. Nice dress. She'll love it.*

I go out into the garden and light a cigarette. The sun has almost set but the sky is still light enough for me to enjoy the irises. And the bougainvillea—thanks to the recent hot spell, the bushes are now more flower than foliage, all startling pink and orange.

A letter came from Amsterdam today. Swee is doing well. New job, textile design. Enjoying himself, parties and everything else. Doesn't say what exactly everything else is, but I don't need to know. At dinner, I tell everyone that he sends his regards. You give me a look. You've always disliked Swee. Too smooth-talking, you say.

Are you going out later? You take my plate and put another helping of rice on it.

Yes. For a while.

Again? Maybe you should think of moving to Amsterdam.

Yeoh

Tiger women, my mother tells me later, are like that. Domineering. Difficult. *Go out if you like. She'll be fine.*

I nod. I decide to stay home. Maybe I will write Swee a letter.

~

Our son is under the bed, crying. This happens every time there is thunder and lightning, and no amount of anything will get him to come out from under it. In the end, we crawl under the bed with him. We put our arms around him and each other and wait for the storm to pass while his sister sleeps, undisturbed by the thunder, the rain, the weeping.

A tiger, a horse, our dog.

A dog child is fiercely loyal. I saw your secret smile when my mother said that. You've never been superstitious, but you loved the thought of an ally, at last.

He is a good boy. Good-natured, easy to please, easy to teach, easy to love. Swee is very fond of him too. *My goodness, he is so much like you. But better looking.*

He is more like you, though. So quick in his movements and in his changes of mood. His laugh is so much like yours. And it was your laugh that made me think, I can marry this girl and live with her. And maybe we'll be friends.

Before the marriage negotiations are final, my eldest sister warns me that you will be too strong for me. *She even reads, because her father let her go to school. A girl like that will think she's too good for us, no matter how poor her family is.*

I don't mind. I want to think that a strong, clever woman will make it easier to do my duty. Every eldest son knows his duties.

~

I don't know what I would have done differently, or if I would have done anything differently. Swee says it is my greatest weakness —my indecisiveness.

But I did decide. I chose you. I chose you and your laugh and your cleverness and our children. You deserve more, but this choice has taken up all I have.

In the end, you chose me too. You stood at your sister's door and you chose me and our son, standing in the storm, and our daughter, sleeping on her thin mattress on the floor in our room. I didn't see him follow me out of the house, but when I felt his hand grab mine in the rain under the umbrella, I was thankful. I knew it would make it easier for you to come home. But I knew you would always come home, and so I chose you.

Dog

They say a boy needs a father. First—please, someone tell me who *they* are. Also, do they really mean a boy needs a father everyone else approves of?

Don't be like your father.

I see you pretending you don't hear it and I'm embarrassed for you. For us. But you ignore it and take me on long walks, you point out the fruit trees and the flowers, you tell me that bougainvillea is native to South America, that in Brazil there are plants exactly like these.

Yeoh

Grandmother says that plants are a waste of time. I must do my homework well, especially mathematics, so that one day I can help in Grandfather's stores.

Don't be like your father.

~

We are on one of our walks, and you stop to examine a vine of bright, blue-purple flowers curling around and over a bush. Uncle Swee, who is not really my uncle, kneels down beside you for a closer look.

Morning glory?

You smile at him. *Yes.*

Aren't they normally a lighter purple?

That's the common variety. These are Japanese.

I come in for a closer look and you point out the petals to me. They are wavy and wonderful, each petal blue with a smear of purple. The flowers are larger than my eight-year-old hand. I pluck a flower to examine it.

Beside me, you and Uncle Swee talk in hushed tones. He seems angry, he waves his arms around. You frown at him and look in my direction.

Uncle Swee turns to me and smiles reassuringly. *It's a pretty flower, isn't it?*

I nod. Uncle Swee turns back to you and the both of you continue to talk, your voices low. He raises his voice a little, and I hear him say: *You need to make up your mind.*

You reply quietly, but he becomes angrier. He walks off without looking back at us.

You get on one knee next to me and you take my hand. The flower falls to the ground. *Growing up will be difficult, you know. Things are easy when you're a child.*

When we get home, Mama gives us an unfriendly look. Where have you been?

The park. You're still holding my hand.

Just the park?

Yes.

Just the two of you?

Yes. You squeeze my hand. I smile and nod at Mama.

She stares at me for a moment, then turns to go back into the kitchen. *After dinner, you better finish your homework.*

~

I have so many stories I would have told you if you had asked, but you didn't and I didn't. But perfect strangers—they will ask anything; they think nothing of the weight of:

How did you two meet?

It's such a natural question to ask a couple. His new colleague smiles encouragingly as she takes another sip of wine.

He reaches for my hand under the table and I let him tell the story. *It was years ago. I was posted to Penang for a short while, and we met at someone's barbecue?*

I nod. I stab at a lettuce leaf.

We went out a few times, but nothing really serious. Then my stint in Penang ended and I came home.

She frowns. *Okayyyyyy. And?*

He smiles. *And then he calls me. Seven years later.*

Seven? She's in her twenties. Seven years is a long time when it's a third of your age.

He's still always late for everything. She laughs. He looks at me and I roll my eyes. *So we talk for hours, and he comes to visit. I thought, this is it. And then I proposed and here we are.*

Oh my God, after seven years? How romantic.

Later, I overhear him tell her: *He didn't come out until his mother died.*

In the kitchen, reaching into the cupboard for more wine glasses, I imagine her eyes widening, her mind working out an explanation for this.

I imagine Ma and her tired eyes and tired face. *Don't be like your father.*

~

I come into the house too quietly. No one hears me. Grandmother and the aunts are in the front room. Mama is out. The door to our room is almost closed—there's a sliver of space between door and doorframe. You're inside and you're not alone.

Uncle Swee is with you, his arms around your shoulders. He's taller and this makes you look small. No one speaks, but your clothes make soft noises like sighs as they fall to the floor.

Later, he gets dressed and combs his hair. *Come with me.*

You shake your head. Uncle Swee leaves. We never see him again.

~

As I turn off the lights, I'm thinking about the night we went to First Aunt's house. I don't remember that much. I remember being scared and wet, I remember you holding my hand.

I remember Mama's cold, angry face at the door. I remember feeling this monstrous wave of guilt, thinking maybe I should have told her what I saw the week before, and this made me cry. I know I called out for her; I know I held your hand and you held mine.

I knew then what we were asking from her; I know now what we asked from you.

He's already in bed. I start to climb in, but something stops me. The window is open and there's a storm coming. I can smell it. I move to close the window, but then I remember you telling me once that it's only water and wind and light and sound, and temporary.

So I leave the window open. I think you would have wanted me to.

Yeoh

SHOPPING FOR BLOUSES

José B. González

In the back of a women's store,
Crystal Mall, another mall, USA.

I'm shopping with my teen girls
again, cell phones at their sides,
they lead me toward a stack
of blouses and then the cash
register. I pull my wallet
from my side, but before I pay,
I ask them to play tag. They
read one aloud,

Women's
S
Made in El Salvador
Hecho en El Salvador

The sewing machines have
been pushed aside to a far-off
world, but I can still hear
their thumping, the drops
of sweat. Their grandmother
touching every stitch.

González

TWO POEMS

Cheswayo Mphanza

(Winner of the 2020 Boston Review *Annual Poetry Contest)*

EDITOR'S NOTE:

I love what Cheswayo Mphanza is doing and asking us to do by centering visual art and film in these two poems. Mphanza is asking us to see what we cannot see as a route to knowing what we cannot know, or to see differently what we think we know. The approach in "Notes Toward a Biography of Henry Tayali"—to start with a painting that the reader cannot see and to move behind it to an image of the life of the artist—is such an exciting poetic take on what biography is. How do we chart life? How do we remember that everything we perceive is something created out of something we cannot see? "Djibril Diop Mambéty Scene Descriptions" asks us to get to the poetics behind and beyond what we see in filmic representation, but also how we envision nation, change, intimacy, and love. Mphanza offers poetry as an agent that causes permeability, allowing these poems to take us so close to the ancestral artists invoked here that we are in their process, we are in their work. We almost become paintings, films, or poems ourselves. But what happens is even better. We, they, all of us remain possible.

—Alexis Pauline Gumbs, 2020 *Boston Review* Annual Poetry Contest judge

Notes Toward a Biography of Henry Tayali

A Pecha Kucha

[*The Village*. Silkscreen Print]

I was born with a language seared on my tongue. I sipped from
the same bottle of pale ale as my father rocked me to sleep. I have
starved a mad dog until it could learn to kneel to me. I have held
a chicken down before my grandmother cleaved its neck clean.
I ate its body whole, sometimes chewing the bones.

[*Bull*. Scrap Metal]

Our summer of love at Victoria Falls. Zamrock the culprit.
Bodies whirling to Paul Ngozi. In the gyre of apartheid further
south and being over the edge of independence. What was
freedom if not our bodies thrust from ourselves and we
trying to catch them in our arrested dances?

[*Regina in My Dreams*. Stencil Sketch]

I pull a petal off a Blue Curiosa and you blossom from its
edges. Bees gossiping around you. The rattle in your legs—
a barefooted dance in white sand. A child's delicate step
on his mother's back. I want to learn to pronounce your body—
enunciate its ridges. Fold your name at the back of my mouth.

Mphanza

[*Untitled*. Oil on Hardboard]

The canvas begins with no paint or name attached. I go back
to my birth in Serenje by the Nsalu Caves. When Zambia was
Northern Rhodesia. My wails winnowed like Wilson's Snipe.
The scene where my father held me as if I was artifact. Rooms
that coated us into primary colors as we tugged against our skin.

[*Herd Boy*. Scrap Metal]

The West was calling my name. Kaunda's dream to show the
African has imagination. I longed for Paris or Florence, but settled
for Germany at Staatliche Kunstakademie Düsseldorf. I learned
their language, read and studied their canon. Caspar David Friedrich
and Adolph von Menzel. For this, I was anointed civilized.

[*People in the Summer*. Oil on Canvas]

At the touch of a paintbrush, or chisel, before I approached the
canvas, block of wood, or scrap metal, my anxiety was that I
saw the body as Western. I was trying to get away from myself
so I turned to the abstract. Hid in the splotches of color coated
bodies to hide beggars, huts, villages, and the African.

[*Unfinished Self-Portrait with Brother Bright Tayali*. Stencil Sketch]

We grind our bodies on the rise. Lick last night's fog from our
lips. Rub the cruel visions captured from our eyes and muzzle
our mouths until screams or swelling moans exhaust themselves.
Recycle the carnage into rage and the courage it needs to blossom;
the dismal loneliness required to live or leave this life.

[*The Other Side of the Bar*. Woodcut]

Sometimes the night is generous and I don't drown as much.
Enough munkoyo courses through me. A drop more and I
pass over to the other side where I become pantomime for my
body strung out at the corner of the bar. Silence subdues me.
I want to leave this country something other than my body.

[*Abstract Painting*. Oil on Canvas]

I was trying to understand my country in the erasure. Women
whose features I did not define and left as polka dots with
head wraps or chitenges around their waists. Was it shame
that defined me? Hiding in the edges of my art to make room
for universal appeal? To be regarded as an artist erased of race?

Mphanza

[*A Measure of Cooking Oil.* Woodcut]

Is modernity shedding ourselves to become exotic fixtures upon lips of critics? *I remain a son of my country. I am a fragment of it. A particle. My art is concerned with the suffering of the people. I want it to be the echo of that suffering. I see the problems of the continent. I am recording what I and my people feel, but I do not attempt to provide answers.*

[Leica SLR Negative Filmstrips]

A child eating cassava. Regina's twisted mouth, cursing me in a mixture of Nyanja, Bemba, and Tonga. David Livingstone's grave. Regina dancing with a white cloth in her left hand. A man burning a kwacha note. A plate of nshima and kapenta. Lusaka at night, littered in variations of light splotches and dark voids.

[*The Beggar.* Woodcut]

I was thinking of the man I saw in Kitwe, resting at the side of a dirt road. He reached his hands to the sky, pretending to fluff one of the clouds before feigning to sleep on it. Maybe he dreamed about finding a country. One not landlocked. His hands outstretched to reach his people. Each of them singing in varied tones of an insatiable hunger.

[*Destiny*. Oil on Canvas]

Realism attempts to render the truth while expressionism is a bad
liar who wants to be honest. This is where I found myself when my
dream of *Destiny* awoke me. It needed to come from the excavated
land I saw Zambia becoming. I took red soil, mixed it with oils and
threw away my watercolors—my fear of their dilution of me.

[*Huts*. Silkscreen Print]

The straw spires send me back to running through fields, brushing
against corn husks. The smell of clay hollow rooms, food laid on mats,
the water bowl we passed to wash our hands. Firewood burning in a
small enclosure. Its blue flames we held all July where we saw winter
pass with a thief's caution, stealing what remained of our warmth.

[*Untitled*. Woodcut]

I see three contours of Regina. All of them the woman I loved and
lost. Gina, is it not you I see in the woodcuts I chisel into effigies?
Their backs shaped like kandolos. Your face, Zambia's best export—
copper. In the mind, I seesaw from the living to your grave. What I'd
give to peel the afterlife's underside to see you under life's awning.

Mphanza

[*Pounding Maize*. Woodcut]

I keep a picture of my mother pounding maize in my front shirt pocket. Photography is best for its simple truth: thought is brief, whereas the image is absolute. This is how I want to remember her: the care in the handle of the falling log; my clinging to her back, wrapped in a chitenge, her movements lulling me to sleep.

[*Lusaka Burning*. Stencil Sketch]

Birds in flight, fleeing their nests. Flapping flames off wings. The Zambezi River a shattered disco ball spitting out shards of crystallized water. Zambia's language milieu where the word for pain is a shared dialect. Nyanja is a fire language, crackling the mouth, and shearing consonants off tongues. What is left is no country, but the imagination.

[*The Omen*. Watercolor]

The moon started to fold into itself. Crows waking at dawn, dusting dusk off their backs. The revelation that stretched my life from star to star. The small thread of a man's life and where he chose to plot and root himself. If I were to weave that thread once more, I wish for more scenes of holding Regina, letting my art be background.

[*The Brothers*. Oil on Canvas]

On a drive through Lusaka, it is W.I.T.C.H.'s tender vibrato that holds me. I know this country tethers us. We will all share the same death. The phantom blood of the '80s which moved our lives at the pace of a stone in a child's hands upon view of open water. The scene that took me back to reading by candlelight until the wick burned into itself.

[*Mother Afrika*. Woodcut]

This country does tether us. A coiled cord pulled from the Zambezi River. Our birthright to our father's tribes, but we are always our mother's children. Bury me here when I inherit the still life of my woodcuts. Smear my ashes on the Nsalu cave paintings. I am thinking of my father who adorned himself griot. I do not worry about legacy—let my art remain.

Djibril Diop Mambéty's Scene Descriptions

We wanted freedom, but we got democracy.
—Hugh Masekela

Scene 1: ESTABLISHING SHOT. The scene must be like a Russian dreaming. Andrei Tarkovsky's mistrust of linearity matched with Mikhail Kalatozov's anxiety of the frame. The camera's demand of austerity. Small incisions of light. A black blank screen. Ominous wails and chatter of Africans rising in the unknown background.

Scene 2: CLOSE UP. Rotating Stills. "The Upright Man" Thomas Sankara adorning a red beret. Kwame Nkrumah, Jomo Kenyatta. Sékou Touré. CUT TO: STOCK FOOTAGE of political propaganda. CUT TO: A-ROLL and B-ROLL of African liberation armies. Coups. Low angle shots zooming into farms being salted. Townships and villages burning. Muddy puddles reflecting the fire. ZOOM OUT: A lush landscape of green. The sky a grainy sienna. CUT TO: Rotating stills of Robert Mugabe: Blaise Compaoré: Paul Biya: Idi Amin: Bokassa standing in front of his bold eagle-styled golden throne. CUT TO: STOCK FOOTAGE. Camera unfolds to a crane view of Lumumba deboarding a plane with handcuffs on his wrists before rope is further tied around his arms. Mobutu in the background. His stare into the camera an anthem collapsing.

Scene 3: WIDE SHOT. Political cartoon of the scramble for Africa. CUT TO: Colonial map of Zambia, then known as Northern Rhodesia. Its edges showing Angola bordering west. DRC northwest. Tanzania northeast. Malawi east. Mozambique southeast. Namibia southwest. Zimbabwe and Botswana south.

Scene 4: A black blank screen with the sound of a train approaching in the background. FADE IN: Mining newspaper the *Nchanga Drum*. On its cover a map showing Northern Rhodesia's Copperbelt railroad line area from Livingstone in the south to the Belgian Congo border. A photograph of white and African miners. Camera zooms into the picture. Entering. The photograph no longer a still setting. Bodies move. White arms and black arms holding pickaxes rise and break in unison against sacred rock. CUT TO: Mining train passing by miners. Zambian women holding their children at the side while selling grain.

Scene 5: CUTBACK: Colonial map of Northern Rhodesia. Kenneth Kaunda's frame growing on top. A litany of abbreviations cut across. ALC; ANC; UNIP; ZANC; ZNBC; UP; UPP; PAFMECSA; PLP; CAA; CAI; CAS; ANIP; AZ; FUCA; MMD; NAZ; UDI; CCMG.

Scene 6: STOCK FOOTAGE of Kaunda on a podium giving a speech at the University of Zambia. "It pays to belong to the UNIP! One Zambia, One Nation, One Country."

Scene 7: WIDE SHOT of Lusaka Independence Stadium. October 23–24, 1964. Zambia army band playing. CUT TO: TIGHT SHOT of the Union Jack waving as it comes down. Zambia's flag ascends. Northern Rhodesia is no more. Zambia is born. Chants from the crowd of "One Zambia, One Nation, One Country!"

Scene 8: MEDIUM SHOT of Zambia's country-side. Morning mist where the trees are covered in rising smoke. CUT TO: Zambezi River. CUT TO: WIDE SHOT of Victoria Falls, showing David Livingstone's statue in Zimbabwe. Dusk falls. FADE OUT.

Scene 9: CLOSE SHOT. The screen unfolds into color, showing a dim room. Two young lovers, both infants of freedom's spring, laying on a straw mattress bed facing a large flag covering the wall. (He doesn't know he has hung the flag backward.) Her head resting on his dead arm. A window open, wind whipping at a loose screw on the side.

Scene 10: CUT TO outside the small room. Though the sky is crowded with storm clouds, the jack snipes don't stop singing. Their song a lisp in the wind. The scene retracts back into black and white. CUT TO inside the room. Blocks of letters spelling out "C-O-P-P-E-R-B-E-L-T P-R-O-V-I-N-C-E." A plastic ornament of an African mask above the bedside table.

Scene 11: MEDIUM SHOT. Static showing on a wooden Zenith television set inside the room before a scene plays from Ousmane Sembène's *Xala* (1975): *Two white men carrying briefcases walk in on a congressional meeting held by African leaders dressed in Western attire. Clapping at the president who resembles Léopold Senghor. He uses words like 'revolutionary' and 'independence' and they garner an applause. The white men place briefcases in front of each leader. They open them and their eyes shine with green. The Léopold Senghor parody rises and announces 'modernity must make us lose our Africanality.' They all clap and disappear with the briefcases into limousines.' TV set goes off.* Camera continues panning around the room of the young lovers. Album poster of Fela Ransome Kuti and The Africa '70's *Confusion* next to Miriam Makeba's solitary stare, turning away from Fela. Facing Papa Wemba instead. (Unbeknownst to the boy, the girl knows something about geography. His abuse of the backward-hung flag.)

Scene 12: TIGHT SHOT. The camera elevates from the bottom of their bed to a parallel scale of the two. The girl reaches for a radio at bedside. Tuning in to Zambia National-al Broadcasting Corporation (ZNBC). Color reenters as Zamrock slowly seeps into the scene. Blackfoot's "Running" plays as their bodies become blurred naked under the stream of moonlight entering through the window. He kisses her belly button—calls it a compass, following its southmost trail. He tells her your skin is beautiful. How one might mistake pollen for cinnamon. She lifts his head gently to her face and kisses him. She says "I'm learning how to take care of flowers. To not worry about the carnations as much as the lilies." He wonders how much less is he in the dark. His mind still in Northern Rhodesia. Landlocked country. "God Save the Queen" still sliding on his tongue when he speaks. She will say she used to belong to a nation, but it kept a record of her raptures so she dissolved it. The moonlight will shine brighter. Revealing parts of his body he wants clothed. He will think "I must possess myself." She will ask what nation he belongs to? His answer her body. A ruthless allegiance. To claim her as country. Call her nation. Carve a kiss on her collarbone and call it a flag. She will tell him independence exacerbates the abrasions of a country. To ask a nation why its flag bears red. The thought of freedom as an open wound. Silence could be useful if he knew its cadence. Maybe the fourth wall should be broken. To invite others into his discomfort. Or maybe they remain as is. Sinking back into bed where he learns making love is immigrating to someone. A citizen who feigns to be a refugee under the tender weight of skin and its nudgings. The unpronounceable pleas of the mouth soaring into an anthem he imagines his. To sustain the borders of her body or coalesce the floor into deep country before they are lulled to sleep. His dream of a nation as suspended and ethereal as her weight next to his. Camera pulls away into a long shot—the focus blurs.

TWO POEMS
Ocean Vuong

The Last Dinosaur

When people ask me what it's like, I tell them
imagine being born in a hospice
that's on fire. As my relatives melted, I stood
on one leg, raised my arms, eyes shut, & thought:
tree tree tree as death passed me—untouched.
I didn't know God saw in us a failed
attempt at heaven. Didn't know my eyes
had three shades of white but only one image
of my mother. She's standing under an ancient
pine, sad that her time on Earth is all she owns.
Oh human, I'm not mad at you for winning
but that you never wished for more. Lord
of language, why didn't you master *No*
without forgetting *Yes*? Sure—we can

make out, if you want, but I'm warning you
it's a lot. Sometimes I think gravity
was like *To be brutally honest* . . . & then
never stopped talking. I guess what I mean
is that I ate the apple not because the man lied
when he said I was born of his rib but
because I wanted to fill myself with its hunger
for the ground, where the bones of my people
still dream of me. I bet the light on this page
isn't invented yet. I bet you never guessed
that my ass was once a small-town wonder.
That the triceratops went nuts
when I danced. How once, after weeks
of drought, I walked through my father's laughter
just to feel the rain. Oh wind-broke wanderer, widow of hope
& ha-has, oh sister, dropped seed—help me.
I was made to die but I'm here to stay.

Nothing

We are shoveling snow, this man and I, our backs coming
closer along the drive. It's so quiet I can hear every flake on
my coat. I used to cry in a genre no one read. What a joke,
they said, on fire. There's no money in it, son, they shouted,
smoke leaking from their mouths. But ghosts say funny things
when they're family. This man and I, we take the weight of

what will vanish anyway and move it aside, making room. There is so much room in a person there should be more of us in here. I wave to you, traveler, inches away but never visible from where I am. Are you warm where you are? Are you *you* where you are? Something will come of this. In one of the rooms in the house the man and I share, a loaf of rye is rising out of itself, growing lighter as it takes up more of the world. In humans, we call this *Aging*. In bread, we call it *Progress*. We're in our thirties now and I rolled the dough just an hour ago, pushing my glasses up my nose with my flour-dusted palm as I read, reread, the hand-scrawled recipe given me by the man's grandmother, the one who, fleeing Stalin, bought a ticket from Vilnius to Dresden without thinking it would stop, it so happened, in Auschwitz (it was a town after all), where she and her brother were asked to get off by soldiers who whispered, *keep moving, keep moving* like sons leading their mothers through wheat fields in the night. How she passed through huddled coats, how some were herded down barb-wired lanes. The smoke from our mouths rising as the man and I bend and lift, in silence, the morning clear as one inside a snow globe. For how can we know, with a house full of bread, that it's hunger, not people, that survives? The man pours a bag of salt over the pavement. But from where I'm standing it looks like light is spilling out of him, like the ray of dusty sun that found his grandmother's hands as she got back on the train, her brother at her side, smoke from the engine blown across the faces outside blurring into pine forests,

Vuong

warped pastures, empty houses with full rooms. The man clutches his stomach as if shot, and the light floods out of him, I mean you—because something must come of this. *Poetry makes nothing happen*, someone who is dead now said after a friend's death. When the guard asked your grandmother if she was Jewish, she shook her head, half-lying, then took from her bag a roll, baked the night before, tucked it in the guard's chest pocket. She didn't look back as the train carried her, newly seventeen, toward where I now stand, on a Sunday in Florence, Massachusetts, squinting at her faded words: *sift flour, then beat eggs until "happy-yellow."* The train will reach Dresden days before the sky is filled with firebombers. More smoke. A bullet in her brother under rubble, his name everywhere outside her like the snow falling on your face forty years later, on December 2, 1984, while your mother carries you, alive only three hours, the few steps to the mini-van where your grandmother, nearly sixty now, crowns your head with her brother's name. *Peter!* she says, *Peter! Peter!* as if the dead could be called back from rubble into new, stunned bones. The snow has started up again, whitening the path as though nothing happened. Oh, to live like a bullet, to touch people with such purpose. To be born going one way, toward everything alive. To walk into the world you never asked for but then choose the room where your hunger ends—which part of war do we owe such knowledge? It's warm in this house where we will die, you and I. Let the stanza be one room, then. Let it be big enough for everyone, even the ghosts rising now from this bread we tear open to see what we've made of each other. I know, we've been growing further apart, unhappy but half full. That clearing snow and baking bread will not save us. I know, too, as I reach across the table to brush the leftover ice from your beard, that it's already water. *It's nothing* you say, laughing for the first time in weeks. *It's really nothing.* And I believe you. I shouldn't, but I do.

A PURSE FULL OF BLACK

Vuyelwa Maluleke

(semifinalist of the 2020 Boston Review *Annual Poetry Contest)*

My tooth is so honest it aches
a howl swarming the bone
a daylight in the body   a fence
trying to pursue a better body for herself.
I wonder if a stronger woman can grow
into the gaps she will leave behind.
& what if all she leaves behind is
a purse full of black and more self-pity

. . . .

And maybe we are not made for very beautiful things, like teeth.

. . . .

People tell me that I am most beautiful when I smile. I smile most
when I am tired, to gain control over my life in public I smile.

. . . .

A father is an army. Or a father is a war.
And during the war the carpet is maroon and you are eight, or twelve,

or sixteen. And only the adults stand in the windows. you are only a daughter so you walk on the bones in your belly to avoid being seen. the carpet files its nails on your skin. you clean the carpet on your knees because the war does not believe in vacuum cleaners. Perhaps you do not own a vacuum cleaner.

I cannot know anymore when I am telling a lie.

The house is always clean. you are always fed. you and your sister play quietly until bedtime: from the bedroom to the kitchen, from the kitchen to the bathroom, from the bathroom to the lounge. you do not look your father in the eyes. you do not talk back. Especially, you must not ask the father if God exists. *Because that is the kind of shit you ask your teachers.*

. . . .

When you cry and the war tells you to stop crying or it will give you something to cry about, you listen and build in yourself a wall so high the sky cannot get in, cannot flood you with anything, not daylight, or rain, or love. One day, when you are still a girl, the father hits you on the hand with a belt and you do not cry. When you do not cry, the father asks you if you think you are a woman now. To get from the woman to the daughter he breaks the skin some more. And when you cry you are his girl again.

. . . .

curiosity is blasphemous.
are you listening?
I need help defending my words.

Maluleke

I need help to say that sometimes I look in the mirror and wonder
if there is another woman in the seams
and will not she live my life for me?
will not she smile for me?
why.
why not.
why will not the body let us lie?

. . . .

I am born so many times.
First I am a girl, then a teacher puts soap in my mouth for saying a
"black word" and then I am Black. One day when I am a Black girl
and know what to do to keep the soap out of my mouth, my body
bleeds out of spite. My aunt who was always a Black Woman tells
me how to wash out the blood. But I cannot wash the pain off the
blood, that must stay. This is woman's work. My aunt tells me to
stay away from pleasure, from chocolate and white pants and boys;
and for a long time I am convinced that pleasure will make me look
fat so I do not allow myself to be touched. I am a Black woman
then. When I am a Black woman I let men touch me because it is
one way to remain untouched. I let men touch me because I am a
woman who loves women and some of the men in my country will
kill you to make you a woman they can love. That is how we love
each other here.

. . . .

Pop Quiz:
If each time that I am born I give up my freedom, what am I?

. . . .

My canines are sharp.
someone says, "why do you need such sharp teeth"
the way that people who think they are revealing something to you ask.
"for people," I say.
I am sharpening my mouth to break through the skin of the emp-
tiness into which I rise.

. . . .

To make sure that the body does not come down stuff the open
spaces with food.

. . . .

Someone measures the wrist
the bracket   the proof
the nod   the obedient government of our hand.
Do other women know to want a body so small it fits around the
horizon of an index finger and a thumb?
have you tried shaking hands with a woman that is dissolving?

. . . .

No one tells you that it is okay to be a color without light. The thing
being born through the thing that is already alive. That you must
bear the scream and know that you are coming.

. . . .

In every poem I am trying to ask a question about a murder:
If I am not touched, how can I know that I am alive?
If my father spends days not speaking, not dying, is he alive?
If I kill myself, will I go to hell?

. . . .

Maluleke

My father fetches the years from the east into the west. My father is a railway man, then a policeman, then a man. But before my father is a man he gives me his east and west to pay for a top row of beautiful teeth. A beauty so crowded it takes years to make straight. Beauty hurts from the time I am twelve until I am seventeen. My mother says that I needed the braces, that without them I would have had an underbite. A face with a drawer always open. Who loves a thing that is always waiting to be filled? In this new face I can hide my want. In this face I look like other girls: shut in and famished, without hunger.

. . . .

This body is work. This body is a needle looking for a damage.

COMPANION ANIMALS
Domenica Ruta

SOMETIME IN MARCH Harriet's fever broke. She got out of bed, changed her shirt, brushed her hair quickly, paddling static into the light thinning strands until they began to stand up and crackle. The snow had melted enough to reveal her muddy Jeep, chewed up by ice, salt, and rust, with a gas tank still full from months ago.

She drove for thirty minutes until she hit the center of town where there were exactly three restaurants, Periwinkles, the Cormorant, and the Weathervane. Everyone had one they went to faithfully, a choice determined largely by ancestry, like a church, and Harriet's restaurant was the Weathervane. She was both looking forward to and dreading the stifling hospitality she would receive there. Yes, it's been a few months now. Yes, thank you. Yes, I'm feeling much better. Oh, thanks. And you? Good, good. Thank you, thank you, yes.

Harriet had been a fixture at the Weathervane her whole life, first as a little girl with her parents on Friday nights, then later, briefly, as a waitress. Everyone agreed she was terribly suited for the service industry, too shy to talk her way into the tips that made heavy lifting and long hours standing around worthwhile. Her parents would come in during her shifts sometimes, and Harriet would seat them in the darkest corner of the restaurant, her face blistering with shame. She would bring them free desserts they never ate and add water to their cocktails.

They died when Harriet was in her early twenties—her father first, dropping suddenly, then her mother two years later, dying a little bit more each day. Harriet had just made her first stab at independence, living hundreds of miles away, but moved back home to help nurse her mother toward that next, uneasy place. She cared for her around the clock sometimes, days without end. Where else was there for Harriet to go then, in those anxious moments of respite after her mother wheezed herself to sleep, but the Weathervane? A decade later she was still going there. It was the first and only place she could think of.

That day Harriet was surprised to see a new waitress working the lunch shift. Her name was Michelle and she'd been hired earlier that winter while Harriet had been sleeping and healing. Michelle was around thirty years old, Harriet guessed, short and curvy with dark bobbed hair and puffy cheeks that made her small eyes practically disappear when she smiled. Michelle smiled a lot. She chatted with Harriet in that breezy way waitresses have, a woman unflappably on your side.

Harriet started coming to the Weathervane regularly, on weekdays after the lunch rush but before the early bird special. The restaurant was slow then and she could take up a whole booth for herself without feeling guilty. When it was sunny and warm, she ordered the Cobb salad, and on rainy or overcast days she had clam chowder in a bread bowl. She never drank anything but water with lemon. Michelle noticed all of this.

"Creature of habit," she smiled as she wrote Harriet's order on her little pad.

"I know," Harriet said. "I'm boring."

Michelle swished a hard candy from one side of her mouth to the other and crushed it between her teeth. "You're just a woman who knows exactly what she wants. Nothing wrong with that, hon!"

The whole human race was *honey* to Michelle, so its diminutive form reached Harriet's ears like a kiss.

Michelle would sit in Harriet's booth when the restaurant was dead. She could have sat at the bar, Harriet noticed, or at an empty table. At her break Michelle collapsed across from Harriet as though the strings that tugged her arms and legs into motion had suddenly been cut, and moaned.

"Rough day?" Harriet asked.

Stretching her legs beneath the table, Michelle rested her feet on Harriet's bench. Her shoes were child-sized and filthy.

"Just give me a razor and a quiet place to bleed," Michelle huffed.

She reached across the table and grabbed Harriet's unopened package of oyster crackers, throwing them into her mouth three at a time. Michelle's eyes were grey with shattered bits of blue. Harriet looked at them for a long time. She felt like she'd arrived somewhere both unrecognizable and familiar.

"Two more weeks until Labor Day," Harriet said. This holiday meant absolutely nothing to her, but she hoped news of it might greet Michelle with cheer.

Ruta

Michelle sank a little deeper into the bench, fanned out a wad of musty green bills from her apron and began counting them.

"I can't wait," she snapped. "All the little college girls will be done pretending to be waitresses for the summer and get the hell out of my hair."

"I never went to college," Harriet offered.

"Really?" Michelle pulled ones and fives out of the stack with a violent flick of her wrist. "I thought all rich people went to college."

"I had dyslexia," she explained. "But I also knew what I wanted to do from a young age, and you don't need a college degree to do it."

Harriet was an equestrian. She'd learned to ride horses around the same time she'd learned to read, planting the knowledge and significance of each equally in her mind. She'd won an Olympic bronze in dressage while still a teenager, and now, when she was well enough to work, made a decent income giving riding lessons at her home, mostly to children as well as a handful of adults. Her parents had left her their house and seventy acres of land when they died, with a stipulation that it could never be sold or developed. She boarded a dozen horses year-round, as well as seven stray dogs. The dogs were also inherited in a way, arriving one by one over the years, usually in the winter.

"It's no accident, these dogs finding you," Michelle said to her. "The animal shelter is so overcrowded they started euthanizing. People take their pets to your farm, instead. You're known around town, Harriet."

"That can't be true."

"Please," Michelle rolled her eyes. "You got a lot of pit bulls, am I right?"

Harriet nodded. She could feel the blood rising into her face. Her skin was thin and milky and it was constantly betraying her. The tiniest bug bite would flare into a bright red welt whether she scratched it or not. Her veins ran so close to the surface that her mother had claimed she could see Harriet's pulse quickening inside her neck.

"People are the worst species alive," Michelle said, sucking her teeth. "This planet is going to scratch us off like a bunch of fleas. And you know what? It'll be better that way."

THE SUNDAY BEFORE LABOR DAY, Harriet invited Michelle on a tour of her stables. Most of the horses she boarded these days were geriatric. Like aging parents in a nursing home, they had been all but abandoned by their owners, wealthy, punctilious people who emailed Harriet regularly but never visited the farm once their horse was settled in. Harriet took care of all the grooming and vet checkups; she fattened the scrawny ones and put the hefty ones on a diet. It was her policy to lay eyes on each of the horses at least once a day. She and Michelle drove around the pastures in an old golf cart, and Harriet called each horse by name.

Carney and Luka shot long sideways glances from their shady spot under an elm. Luka trotted over when Harriet called him, but Carney, eyeing Michelle, remained close to the silent, voluptuous tree. Rowan, the chestnut mare, was easily bribed with a handful of oats, but when Michelle tried to stroke her neck, she sneezed haughtily and ran away.

Ruta

"I'm sorry," Harriet touched Michelle's shoulder lightly and then pulled her hand away, as though testing the temperature of a kettle on the boil. Michelle took her hand back and squeezed it.

"I'm tougher than I look, hon."

All of the horses had free range of Harriet's land except for the oldest three, Holly, Lazarus, and Coltrane. They slept inside a stable and spent their days in the paddock nearest Harriet's house. Coltrane was a retiree from Suffolk Downs. His owners insisted he get an expensive store-bought feed, Harriet told Michelle with a little snort, though he'd eat anything you could put in a bucket.

"He'd gobble up wood chips and not know the difference, I swear."

Lazarus was twenty-nine and had respiratory problems. He was the only one Harriet kept blanketed, and she mixed corn oil in his feed. Holly didn't need anything except hay, but because she was pastured with the other two, Harriet left a scoop of Coltrane's feed in her bucket.

"It just kills me," Michelle said. She gave Lazarus a good scratch on his withers. "No one gives animals the credit they deserve."

Harriet's house was furnished exactly as it had been before she was born. Every five years she touched up the exterior paint, a stately white with dark green shutters. When she was healthy enough, she did most of the painting herself. Inside, the house was neat and very dusty. Michelle picked up a photo from the mantle over the fireplace. It was a picture of Harriet, aged twelve. She peered at the camera with the same brown, bovine eyes she had now, the same limp blond hair drawn like curtains to reveal her diffident smile. Michelle wiped the dust off the picture with her sleeve.

"Aww. You were old even when you were young. You even got an old lady name," she observed. Harriet's face prickled. There was a shame in being seen by another as she saw herself. She didn't know how to respond. Before she could decide, Michelle said, "Your parents were big drunks, weren't they?"

"They liked their scotch," Harriet admitted.

"Mine too."

MICHELLE SPENT THAT NIGHT at Harriet's house and two weeks later moved in. This new girlfriend had a stable of her own, Harriet soon learned, and it was full of exes, men and women from the Weathervane whom Harriet had never noticed in all her years eating there, and then many more friends and lovers who would drive all the way from Boston and Portland and Provincetown to spend the evening with them. They were rich, effusive people whose lives all seemed to unhinge without a regular dose of Michelle's blithe attention. They arrived unannounced as the sun set, bringing old and new significant others in tow, and big jugs of wine or loaves of zucchini bread from the farmers market down the road. They made themselves at home with an ease that suggested some troubling facts: *home* was wherever Michelle happened to be, and Michelle moved around a lot.

"Harriet, you should buy a llama," Darah said one night. She was a lawyer and a competitive poker player with dark, dramatic eyebrows. "You won't believe the tax break you'd get just for having a single animal deemed *exotic*. Peacocks fall into that category, too, I think."

Harriet nodded dumbly and felt her face with her hands. A low-grade fever was coming on.

"Forget the llamas. With a kitchen like this, you're crazy not to turn this place into a B&B," suggested Colette, a former model who seemed to do nothing now. "Is the basement finished? How many bedrooms do you have?"

Every other night these people came, shameless as barn cats in the way they rubbed up against Michelle, begging for affection that she doled out in generous, uneven helpings. By the end of the fall, Harriet was exhausted.

"I have a lot of people who love me, hon," Michelle said as they stripped the sheets off one of the guest beds. "I haven't been very lucky in another way but that."

"I just don't like it when your friends start telling me what to do. This is my house. They make me feel like all my opinions are wrong."

"That's not true, hon. Everyone loves you. They think you're the best. Even Bryce said so, and he never compliments anyone."

Bryce was a dividends trader with muscular arms and tiny hands. He could be relied on to show up with venison or something else he had recently killed. Harriet wanted to like him, she sincerely tried, but he was always trying to convince Michelle that she should go back to school. There was an urgency in these appeals that seemed to say more about him than her. He didn't so much as acknowledge the dogs who nosed in and out of their late-night dinners. "Your pasture ornaments," he called the horses grazing the fields.

"They're companion animals, both to me and to each other," Harriet said. It had taken weeks of silent rehearsals to say this to him.

Bryce uncorked another bottle of wine. "You're just anthropomorphizing," he said.

"Then why does Ginger smile whenever she sees me?"

"It's not a smile. It's the conditioned response of a parasite that senses its food source is near. Dogs are the most successful parasites in the world. They evolved in accordance with our narcissism. We see ourselves in the whites of their eyes," he said grandly. "Sclera and the illusion of eye contact. I'd say dogs were brilliant if they weren't so dumb."

There was a single crease running horizontally across his forehead, straight and rigid as a scar. It deepened when he got argumentative, which was whenever he drank, which was always.

"Put a mirror in front of a dog or cat, even a monkey, and it recognizes nothing," he pronounced.

"Some things don't need to be recognized like that," Harriet said. Her joints ached and she felt like she was going to cry. "They don't have anything to prove."

Animals played and fought and loved and dreamed. They made choices that had nothing to do with instinct or survival. Harriet was surer of this than any other fact in her life. Gemini, the palomino, would come to the defense of younger horses in her pasture but horses who were older she let fend for themselves. When the German shepherd Biff had to be put down, Paulie the terrier forsook his pile of blankets on the kitchen floor and slept outside for one night. Paulie circled the spot under the forsythia where Biff liked to bury his tennis ball and buried one of his own, an act the dog had never performed before and never since.

Ruta

"If that's not a grief ritual, I don't know what is," Harriet said.

"Bryce is just flirting, hon."

Michelle scooped some vanilla ice cream into a bowl and offered it to the new scrawny pit bull lurking warily at the edge of the patio. The dog darted away as soon as she came near. A silence descended around the table. For a moment the only sounds were the settling of ice in people's glasses, the *chick* of Michelle's lighter and the crisp, intermittent burning of her cigarette. In the distance two dogs were barking. Michelle massaged Harriet's shoulder. She kissed her neck. Her breath was warm with the smell of beer.

"It's such a nice night," she said. "We're not going to have too many more like this. Let's fire up the grill. I'm in the mood for ribs."

LESS THAN A YEAR LATER, Michelle left Harriet for a married man whose table she served at the Weathervane. She phoned Harriet from the restaurant, the clanging of dishes and the din of conversations rumbling behind her.

"We're moving to Florida. Armand owns a couple gas stations down there. I'm going to work for him, doing the books and stuff."

Harriet felt her legs go numb. She sank into a chair. The phone burned inside her hand. As though in a trance, she opened the newspaper with her other hand, to an article she had already read, about deer in Essex County becoming addicted to nicotine. Apparently, hunters had been dropping their cigarette butts in the forest and the deer began to eat them, filters and all. Over the course of one hunting season, the deer had lost their appetites and become irritable.

"What? What?" Harriet said. Her hands shook now and felt very far away.

"I'm so sorry, hon. I really am. It just happened. You don't have to do anything. Just throw my stuff in a box and leave it in the mud-room. I'll come by to pick it up eventually. Harriet? Are you there? I said I was sorry."

"I heard you the first time."

FOR WEEKS Michelle's exes still came to the house looking for her. It was impossible for Harriet to contact them all and report Michelle's new address, her new life. The exes were all saddened to learn she had gone though not the least surprised. They returned to Harriet's farm in the evenings like before, bringing their wine and cheese, sitting on the patio as though expecting their prodigal waitress to return. A meteor shower was expected for the end of August and someone decided that Harriet's house on an unlit country road offered the best view. A party was planned and Harriet surrendered almost instantly, holding on to the dim hope that Michelle might show up, her heart and mind changed.

Bryce was the first to arrive that Sunday night as the sun was beginning to set. He carried a slightly dirty blender under his arm. He made a lot of noise pushing appliances around the kitchen counter as he searched for an outlet. Harriet watched him get out the cutting board and begin slicing a watermelon into cubes.

Ruta

"Is this the sharpest knife you have?" he asked.

"Check in the—in the drawer—over there." She was exhausted. The newspaper she had opened the day Michelle left her was still on the table, open to the same page. There was a picture of a man in a florescent orange cap offering a pack of Marlboros to the carcass of a buck he'd killed.

"You know what I was thinking on the ride over? You should really open a petting zoo here. I could back you on the initial investment."

He cracked an ice tray so violently the plastic tore on one side. "Cheap thing," he muttered. Harriet sat at the dining room table, her head and hands aching as she stared through the large bay window at the sky. It was a lonesome blue with a stripe of pink clinging to the horizon just above the trees.

Darah and her new girlfriend, Kris, drove onto the lawn in a Jeep stripped of doors, roof, and windshield. They brought a blood-filled plastic bag of steak tips, several unripe avocados, and six bottles of red wine. Four friends of theirs parked behind them and sang arm in arm as they walked up the driveway. Did these people even know who Michelle was, Harriet wondered. An hour later a man Harriet had never seen before made his way up the driveway. He somehow knew without ever having met her that Harriet was the owner of the house and introduced himself as Kenny, a friend of Michelle's.

"I don't know what's left for food," Harriet sighed. "Steak. Maybe some salad?"

"I'm OK, thanks. All I need is some shooting stars," Kenny said. He'd brought his own folding chair, which he set up next to the thoroughbred's paddock.

A speck of light began to wiggle and fall from its spot in the sky. The one seemed to trigger another, then another, until meteors like tiny white fish began darting across a great black sea.

Kenny giggled to himself. "What a show," she heard him say.

It wasn't long before most of the guests stopped looking at the sky and moved inside the house to be closer to the blender of watermelon margaritas. Kenny remained seated in his chair. There was a solemnity to the way he smoked his cigarettes that Harriet found calming. They sat together without speaking, their heads tilted awkwardly like people in the first row at a movie theater.

Bryce, Darah, and Kris had all passed out in the living room. Harriet went inside to wake them and assist with the inevitable fracas of finding purses, keys. The blender was leaking pink juice onto the counter. It dripped down a cabinet and onto the floor, where a trail of black ants marched to meet it. Kenny began collecting glasses and utensils to rinse in the sink. He squeezed out a yellow sponge and wiped the juice off the cabinets.

"I was kind of hoping she would show up tonight," Kenny said, his back toward Harriet. "She was happy here. You were good for her, I think."

"Did she do this to you, too?" Harriet blurted. "Did she move in and make you feel like she'd always been there, then disappear like nothing even happened?"

"Wasn't like that. I was trying to help her get sober. I used to drive her around and let her talk. We went to meetings sometimes together. When she could stand it. But that's all."

"I'm sorry," Harriet said, wiping her eyes with the backs of her hands. "I just miss her so much."

Ruta

"I know."

"Was she using me? Or do you think she actually loved me? I can't tell anymore."

"I think she means what she says when she's saying it. Sometimes I believe she really does want to get better. She's sincerely tried to. A couple of times. But I don't know. A long time ago I stopped trying to understand how other people think."

Kenny wiped the dishes with a rag, then hung the rag to dry on a bent nail jutting out of the wall. He let his hand fall gently to the top of Harriet's head and, for a brief moment, the pain in her skull burnt away like dew in the morning sun.

"I might check in on you, from time to time. Would that be all right?"

"Please," Harriet said, her eyes streaming. "Please do."

SUMMER COOLED TO FALL. Blasts of yellow, orange, and red lit up the trees. Harriet looked forward to this exact time of year, when the wind picked up the smell of decay and carried it sweetly through the air. But the fall after Michelle left, she was so sick she could hardly spare the strength to smile. The half-empty bed, the crush of souls drifting around the patio, the anger and the hopeless grief, all these things, the doctors told her, were the obvious stressors that had made Harriet's lupus come out of remission.

Her pain had a luminous quality, both particle and wave, glowing brightest in the places where bone met bone. Folding laundry, writing a check—these acts had to be done early in the day, before the pain got unbearable, or not at all. Every morning she rose no later than six and drove out to the pastures wearing a stained white nightgown and a pair of jeans. After that she had an hour, two if she was lucky, before she would collapse.

"I'll soak in a salt bath," she said as she dragged a brush across Lazarus's gleaming hide. Her wrists started to hurt and she shook out her hands as though cooling them from a burn.

She didn't shower, some nights didn't bother to take off her boots before dropping off to sleep. Some nights began in the early afternoon. She stopped giving lessons after a rash like scarlet wings broke out across her face. When Michelle's friends saw her now, they were apologetic and quick to leave.

"You need anything?" the nicer ones offered, their voices straining under the hope that she didn't. Harriet's rash made people try too hard to look her in the eyes, an effort that was conspicuous and kind and never failed to make her feel worse.

"No, thank you," she answered.

Everything she needed she could get delivered, and so she seldom left the house. She fired her small staff and spoke to no one except her doctors, the farrier, and the mobile vet.

It was a surprise then to hear the twinkling of her cell phone buried beneath a pile of unopened mail. Harriet was in the kitchen boiling a chicken carcass into stock. She squinted at the screen. "BOSTON COURTHOUSE," the caller ID said in all capital letters, as though commanding her to answer.

"Harriet, it's Kenny. What are you doing today? Can you come down to my office this morning?"

Ruta

Inexplicably, Harriet heard herself saying yes.

He met her on the front steps, his hands chapped and dry as he lit a new cigarette with the red orb of the one he had just finished.

"Hang out in my office and read the file. Later, if you want to meet him, I can arrange it. No pressure. I just think he would love it at your place. All those animals. Perfect place for a kid like him."

He was a baby, in fact, not a kid. His name was Josh, a plump, brown-eyed toddler, currently a ward of the state. One day while Josh's mother was out chasing drugs, someone, it was not clear who, had shaken him until he went into seizures. Someone else had brought him to the hospital but no one came to pick him up.

He was sucking on a face cloth when Harriet finally met him in Kenny's office. The baby wouldn't look at her. His eyes were dark and dim, like windows whose glass had been painted over. A satiny scar forked through his hair like a pale river.

"Can I think about it? Maybe sleep on it a night?"

"Absolutely," Kenny said. "And it would only be temporary. You're not adopting him. Just fostering him. His mother could come back for him any day now, and she has rights. He's special needs, so he's been a tough little guy to place for the short term."

It was miraculous what a man like Kenny could do simply by picking up the phone. Harriet imagined the little machine sitting on his desk glowing with magical light. How else could this have happened, she wondered, if not by modes of enchantment? She had left her house that morning with nothing but a wallet and was returning with a child, a baby boy, in her arms.

JOSH BEGAN TO WHIMPER in his high chair. Harriet hummed at him, spooned some oatmeal from the pan and pushed it toward his mouth. The pale grey mush dropped down his bib in one chunk. "OK, no more oatmeal," Harriet conceded. Every meal was a new experiment. Josh was nearly two and he would never learn to talk or walk. His skull was fractured into minutely shifting plates that the doctors told Harriet would be vulnerable for the rest of his life, a short wink of time at best. Josh's sense of taste was the only thing Harriet felt sure she understood. He loved both red and green grapes as well as all varieties of cheese. Popcorn and boiled carrots he spat out as though offended. Peanut butter and apples he would eat but not together. So far she'd had no luck with raisins but was still trying.

It was almost eight in the morning and she still hadn't gotten a bite of food into the boy. Harriet took away the oatmeal and offered Josh a piece of banana. He batted it away and began to howl.

"What do you want? Please tell me."

The baby slapped himself in the face. Such tiny, delicate hands. His fingernails were so small it scared her a little, and she thought, this is what love is—something terrifying that you don't have the heart to be afraid of.

Harriet lifted Josh out of his high chair and wrapped him in his favorite towel. She offered him everything in her kitchen but he just twisted away from it. Finally she sat him on the cool tiles under the kitchen table. It had calmed him in the past though not always. She extended a slice of rye bread toward his hand, and watched his little fist unfurl and take hold. He held the bread in his hand, his eyes rolled upward. She gave him another slice of bread, one for each hand to hold, and slowly his cries began to soften. Josh moaned apologetically. His nostrils flared and the tears subsided.

At the door, one of the dogs began to whimper. It was the mean little Jack Russell, the one who nipped. Since Josh arrived, Harriet had kept all seven dogs outside. Some were taking this better than others. The five pit bulls roamed the pastures and pretended to herd the horses. But Jack had formerly belonged to the inside caste, lazing on his chosen corner of the living room couch; he had been excommunicated and he knew it. He scratched at the door, his yelping baleful and sharp.

Josh heard these cries and his face pinched with the threat of more tears.

"You just hold on to those for me, OK?" Harriet said. He gripped the bread slices and watched her face for the next thing.

HARRIET AND JOSH both had doctor's appointments on the twenty-first of April. It was a long day full of waiting and discouragement. The kidney transplant that Harriet had been avoiding her whole life had at last become necessary and urgent. Josh was not getting better, but then again, he never would. Harriet was looking forward to a nap when they got home, but sitting on the bottom step of the porch was Michelle.

She stood up slowly as Harriet got out of the car. She was wearing a pair of blue hospital scrubs held up with safety pins and a T-shirt so billowing it didn't seem to touch her body.

"Hi," she said.

Her arms dropped around Harriet's neck. They kissed dryly on the mouth. Michelle's hair was down to her waist and her nails were all broken or bitten to the quick.

"I've been waiting since ten in the morning. I'm so hungry."

"I made egg salad last night. It's in the fridge."

"Oh, thank you!" Michelle burst into tears. "Thank God."

She ate wolfishly, her hands trembling as she drained glass after glass of orange juice. When she was finished, she leaned back from the table and began to light a cigarette.

"Oh, sorry," Harriet said, waving her hand gently, "we can't smoke inside anymore."

"At all?"

"No, sorry."

Harriet swept her gaze over to Josh, who was still sleeping in his car seat in the middle of the kitchen table.

"You mind going on the porch?"

"Of course not, hon."

She watched Michelle through the window walking up and down the gravel driveway. A purple band of light slung low over the trees. The orb of her cigarette bobbed from her waist to her lips. The dogs came, one after another, and surrounded her. A pit bull dropped a filthy length of rope at her feet. Michelle picked it up and threw it weakly down the hill. The dogs scrambled after it and returned again and again. Harriet could see her lips moving. Was she talking to the dogs or to herself, she wondered. Michelle lit another cigarette, throwing the rope up and down the driveway, whispering to herself in the falling dark.

Ruta

THE NEXT MORNING Harriet awoke to the smell of coffee brewing downstairs.

"I'm taking orders," Michelle said brightly. "What can I make you? Eggs? Pancakes? You name it."

"I'll have whatever you're having."

Harriet sat Josh on her lap and fed him from a jar of apples she'd cooked down to a mash. Michelle laid strips of bacon onto a frying pan. It crackled and hissed.

"Ow!" Michelle jumped back. "It's spitting at me."

"Turn down the heat a little."

"Motherfucker," she yelped. "Why does your frying pan hate me? Look."

She thrust her elbow toward Harriet and pointed to the light pink burn.

"Run it under some cold water," Harriet said and fed another spoon of apples to Josh. Michelle shut the stove off and slammed the pan onto the counter. She left to smoke a cigarette on the back porch. When she returned, she dropped the newspaper on the table. It was still encased in its blue plastic sleeve and dripping with last night's rain.

"I need to get my stuff, Harriet. I'd like to get that over with today."

Her belongings, she explained, were scattered over a few locations. Some of her things were in a storage facility the next town over. "And some are at Armand's old house," she said, pulling a fresh cigarette from her pack. "His ex-wife still lives there, I think."

"Can you please do that outside?"

"Oh, sorry." Michelle moved toward the screen door which she held open a crack with her foot.

"Do you want me to come with you?" Harriet offered.

"Yes and no." She released a string of smoke from her mouth that twisted then vanished before her face.

"How about I drop you and the baby off somewhere and then I take your car and just get it done fast? After we can go out or something. I don't know. We should do something to celebrate."

"Perfect," Harriet said, struggling to open a window with her one free hand. "Drop us at the library and after we'll all go out to eat. Josh loves restaurants."

The children's room at the public library hosted a storyteller on the first Friday of every month. Sometimes Josh would cry too loudly and Harriet would have to leave. That day he laid peacefully in Harriet's lap for the duration of the story. Afterward the other moms and their children drifted toward the circulations desk and then out the door. They chatted with each other but never with her. Dogs and horses would at least sniff in curiosity. What must they think of us, she wondered. The other mothers probably didn't think of them at all, she decided. What did Josh think of her, she wondered instead. What parts of her would he take with him when their time together was over?

Ruta

WHEN MICHELLE FINALLY ARRIVED, she was crying, her face bright red as though it had recently been slapped.

"What happened?"

"I don't want to talk about it. Can we please just get something to eat?"

The Weathervane was out of the question. Michelle said she wanted Chinese, so they drove an extra thirty minutes to Fortune II. As soon as they were seated, Michelle ordered a Long Island iced tea. Harriet asked for water with lemon and no ice.

"Come on. Get a drink with me."

"I don't want to pay for something I'm only going to sip twice."

"Don't worry about that, hon. I'll finish it for you."

Harriet ordered a light beer. Michelle raised her glass to her.

"Over and onward, my love."

Harriet felt an exquisite pain take over her body as they clanked glasses. This is it, she thought for a moment. My heart is stopping. My kidney is shutting down. This is the end of me, right here, right now.

The pain retreated for a moment, sucked backward like water drawn under the tide. She wasn't dying, not now anyway. She saw Michelle drain her glass then twist in her seat to call the waitress for another. Harriet pulled Michelle's arm down.

"No, sweetheart. Can we leave? I don't feel good."

"Come on. Just a little longer? It's not even seven o'clock."

"I'm getting a fever. I can feel it."

"No, you're not," Michelle pleaded. She pressed her palm against Harriet's sweaty cheek. "You're fine, hon. You look good."

"I need to get him home. It's time for his bath."

"What does it matter if he takes a bath later? He'll never know the difference. And I thought it was your fever that was the problem."

"I need us, all three of us, to go home."

HARRIET WOKE EARLY the next morning. The moment her feet hit the cold wood floor, she felt it—the bleak elation that surfaces when what you are doing is either exactly right or exactly wrong. Michelle was snoring, her face tipped back and her eyes squinted as though bracing herself for something in her dreams. Josh lay supine in his specially designed bed, his hands balled into little empty fists. Downstairs Harriet looked through the window into the mudroom where the dogs now slept. Her breath made a small, reassuring circle on the glass. Everyone was here, accounted for, alive.

She went to the cellar and emptied the dryer. A pair of jeans ripped to strings, a few pairs of socks and a few thongs, all of it still warm to the touch. Tears fell down Harriet's face as she folded Michelle's clothes. The skin on her cheeks was raw still, a good month or two away from being healed. She moved quietly around her house, collecting all Michelle's discarded belongings, then loaded everything into a shopping bag that she put in the back seat of the car alongside the rest of her things hauled out of storage.

WEEKS LATER Josh had a seizure that left his right eye sagging. "Petit mal," Harriet explained to him. "That means small-bad. Not big-bad. Not yet."

They sat together on the kitchen floor and opened a box of mail-order prescriptions. Michelle was gone but Harriet's immune system was still a mangy dog chewing its own tail. She was trying naturopathy, fish oils, and foul-smelling herbs dissolved in hot water. So far nothing had worked.

She lined up all her new medicine bottles according to size, shaking each one near Josh's ear, and if he liked its percussion, she would offer it to him to shake. Josh was much more interested in the foam packing peanuts spilling out of the cardboard box. They were everywhere, a curious little storm, sticking to their heads and arms and hands and shirts, floating in static repulsion like snow.

"ROOM, ROOM, ROOM, IN THE MANY MANSIONS OF ETERNAL GLORY FOR THEE AND FOR EVERYONE"

–The Archangels to Publick Universal Friend upon the Friend's first death

Day Heisinger-Nixon

(*finalist for the 2020* Boston Review *Annual Poetry Contest*)

When the Friend emerges, they refuse a name & report they have died at least once. The doctor, god of the bone hammer & other phalluses, says *NoNoNo that's just the decaying room.*

In America, we have bones & kidneys & other things we pay to see. My doctor, the conceptual artist, presents *The Bones in Ur Body R Grinding Together* & I applaud in the examination room.

Wary of the doctors, the apple prays *Please denude me* & I help her slip from her thin skin. My grandma has thin skin & fainting spells & calls to confirm my symptoms from the waiting room.

Wary of herself, my grandma pleads to the doctor through a child's child, *Tell me who I am.* The child's child talks low, does not give on to the doctor, considers this a form of making room.

Back on earth, god of the bone hammer & other phalluses wikipedias *collagen* to determine the cause of the fainting spells, says, *The tests are boring for everyone; you'll just be taking room.*

LA is a place where you can choose one age & be it forever. I choose to be root-rot old & pass the long-horned bees into the long-grained grass which makes way to a long-forsaken room.

The patterns on my genes & on my mothers' are a bit derivative. Once, while napping along the shore of a river, I dreamt of a river, only to find myself impossibly redundant upon waking. Rumi writes *The wound is the place where the Light enters you.* Light writes her name on all that has been forced to lose its own. Light loves the room, lays her palms along her ribs, breaking room.

_____

Note: Publick Universal Friend (b. 1752) was an American Quaker who fell ill and was reported dead before being reanimated as a "genderless evangelist prophet." This poem considers, in the light of the Friend, the confluence of gender and illness, and a sick trans American ancestry.

ON ANONYMITY

Bennet Bergman

(finalist for the 2020 Boston Review *Annual Poetry Contest)*

We knew so little about the plague we underwent
Fresh-named
Even now I must review it

In life I had been stripped   sucked   paid for   scraped
In every Atlantic seaboard town
Sex was my green trapeze   my scanty armor

I preferred men   the gendered accoutrement
Of the French-Canadian duo   their arms around me
The way a bachelor fellow   if he loved you
Would tie your wrists to a high branch with a thousand knots

Beauty   the betrayer
Was a mountain I moved through   my first and last muse
To have adored an ass   an old man   a roomful of people

I worked hard to erase the heavy netting strung between
One stranger at a time   O you must dissolve inside me

According to early reports the first cases took hold in the most promiscuous
So no one stands on a rug that cannot be pulled out from under him
I have been waiting to say this   I'm waving my arms now
Courage   dignity   a forced bloom
You do not belong to the family you believe you belong to

———

Note: "On Anonymity" *is an erasure poem. The source text,* Anonymity *(1994), was written by my late mother, Susan Bergman. Reviewer Meg Wolitzer described the book as "a stark and angry account of the death of the author's father from AIDS and the family's subsequent uncovering of his covert homosexuality." Original word order has been preserved and words have not been added or altered.*

ONWARD

STRAIGHT DOWN TO THE BONES

Sonia Sanchez interviewed by Christina Knight

A KEY FIGURE in the Black Arts Movement and a founder of Black Studies, Sonia Sanchez has authored more than a dozen books of poetry, criticism, and plays. Though I've never met Sanchez in person, it is not an exaggeration to say that her life as a poet, playwright, and professor has made my own possible. Taking a class on the Black Arts Movement as an undergraduate introduced me to the fire behind her language. My graduate training in African American Studies showed me images of her as an impossibly young professor, fighting for the establishment of Black Studies at San Francisco State University. And most recently, in my own life as a young professor in Philadelphia, I've seen Sanchez enter a room and be suddenly surrounded by former students, friends, and colleagues, living evidence of her lifelong generosity of spirit. Sanchez radiates brilliance, humor, and integrity, and her work has touched countless lives.

It was a joy, then, to speak with her about the many people, living and dead, who have shaped her own journey. In our interview, she discusses mentors and teachers as well as her fierce devotion to her students. She concludes by recalling her writing process for *A Blues Book for Blue Black Magical Women* (1974), an astonishing volume of poetry shaped by the artist's dream dialogues with her late mother.

—Christina Knight

CHRISTINA KNIGHT: You have stated that there are lots of people, of various ethnic and racial backgrounds, who have inspired you and your own vision for a more just and peaceful world. Could you talk about who some of those people are—those chosen ancestors—who guide you on your journey?

SONIA SANCHEZ: Some of them are people like Jean Hutson, who was a curator and then chief of the Schomburg Center for Research in Black Culture for decades. When I was finishing my bachelors at Hunter College, at the end there was a season between when I finished my course work and when I would officially graduate in January. So my dad said, "Well, you'd better go out and get a job." Someone I was talking to said, "Why don't you look at the *New York Times*? They have all of these ads." So I looked and there was one for a writer for a firm. And I thought why don't I, at that point, play with what I really want to be?

I sent an application and I got a telegram on Saturday that said to report to work on Monday; I was hired. So on Monday I went out in my blue suit, and my hat, and my blue pumps, and my blue bag. I went out like a church person, you know what I mean? I got there at 8:30, and eventually this woman came up to me and said, 'Can I help you?'" So I took the telegram out and handed it to her. I remember she read it, and then she looked up at me. Then she handed it to me and said, "Come in and have a seat." So I'm sitting there, and a man walks in and says, "Yes, can I help you?" I had my letter out, and I handed it to him. And he read the letter and looked at me. And you know, I am smiling the whole time. And he handed it back to me and said, "I'm sorry, the job is taken."

I said, "I understand. This is about discrimination, and I'm going to report you to the Urban League." He turned around and shrugged like, "Lady, I don't care who you report it to." I remember going all the way to the subway with tears in my eyes. In New York City, if you want to stay on the West Side, you have to get off at 96th Street to make sure that you get that West Side train. Well, all of a sudden, the door closes, and I realize that I missed my stop; and then that train shifts over to the East Side, where it starts to shake, and you think it's going to collapse. It feels like it's having a nervous breakdown.

I knew that if I was going to the Urban League to report this, I had to get up in the 130s, so I got off at 135th Street, across the street from Harlem Hospital, and started walking west. About a fourth of the way down the block there's just a little building that says "Schomburg Library." There's a guy out there smoking, so I looked up and I said, "What is the Schomburg?" And he said, "Miss, go inside, sign in, and walk up the steps. There's a lady in there, and she'll tell you." I went inside, signed in, went up the steps, and got to this place where there was an amazingly long table, and nothing but Black men were sitting there with books stacked up—scholars, right? Their heads were down, and they never looked up. To the right of that was this glass door. I knocked on the glass door, and the door opened. I said "Hello," and I introduced myself. And she says, "My name is Jean Hutson." So, I said, "Miss Hutson, what kind of library is this?" And she said, "My dear, this library has books only by and about Negroes." And me and my fresh mouth said, "So there must not be many books in here, huh?"

In my teaching career, I would always bring my students to the Schomburg to do research and to meet her also. Every time I brought my students, she'd tell that story: she'd say, "I have a story to tell you about your professor." I'd move to the back, and after she'd finish, my students would say, "Ooo, I've got something on you now."

But anyway, there we were. So she went, and she asked the men to move over; she pulled up a chair, and she said, "Just sit down, and I'm going to bring you some books." Fifteen or twenty minutes later, she comes back with Booker T. Washington's *Up from Slavery* (1901), W.E.B. Du Bois's *The Souls of Black Folk* (1903), and Zora Neale Hurston's *Their Eyes Were Watching God* (1937). She said, "Just look these over," and she went back into her office. I started with *Their Eyes Were Watching God*.

As I kept reading, my eyes and my mouth became accustomed to the Black English. You really do have to stretch yourself, because although we did use some Black English in our home, we never saw it written. So, there I was struggling with it. And then I started to get some rhythm, and then I had to get up again. I remember easing my way out and knocking on the door.

I said, "How could I be a graduate in New York City and never come across this book?"

"I know," she said, "I'm going to give you lots and lots and lots of books." And that began the training. I would tell my father I was looking for a job, and I would come down there, take my hat off, put my coat over the chair, and begin to read again. There I was, every day, supposedly looking for a job.

Later Hutson sent me to Lewis Michaux's African National Memorial Bookstore on Seventh Avenue, as well as to Richard Moore's Frederick Douglass Book Center on West 125th Street, which was so small you had to go in sideways. Each one of them gave me grocery bags of books. And that is why I say to you simply: This woman was certainly one of the people that I would talk about with great respect and great love. But there's also Martin Luther King, Jr., and Malcolm X, and Medgar Evers, and Gwendolyn Brooks, who was an amazing writer but also a supporter of young writers—she was always giving an award to us, you know, in the form of some money to keep us going. Margaret Walker, Sterling Allen Brown, of course; and contemporaries Amiri Baraka and Joy Hakim.

CK: But I love that it all started with Jean Hutson, that day when you walked into the Schomburg.

SS: And from that motion and movement there, from reading those books, Black books. That took me to people like Shirley Graham Du Bois, who became my mentor, later, when I was at Amherst College. She was at the University of Massachusetts working on W. E. B. Du Bois's papers, and she was at my house almost every night. I would feed her, and she would keep me up. I would put my twins in the bathtub, and they would flood the floor, while we talked downstairs and ate together. She really introduced me to international Blackness, and through that I came to be in dialogue with the work of people like Ngũgĩ wa Thiong'o and Chinua Achebe.

But I'm also a writer of haiku and have been influenced by Japanese writers such as Bashō. And then people like Howard Zinn, whose teaching about progressive politics at Spelman College impacted Alice Walker and so many others. And of course the Beat poets, such as Allen Ginsberg. All of these people helped teach me how to become the poet who I needed to be.

I remember a period when I was young and trying to take graduate classes taught by famous New York poets, but I would go in and the entire class would be twelve or thirteen white men. And the teacher, the poet, would also be a white man, and I was the only Black woman there. I'd sit there and I'd sometimes make a comment, and no one would acknowledge the comment that I had made. So after about the third session I left. That happened twice.

But then I saw that Louise Bogan, poetry reviewer for the *New Yorker*, was teaching a class I hadn't registered for, but I went anyway and when she arrived she said, "Good afternoon," even though it was night, and she said that the class would be focused on form. The whole group moaned, because we were free verse people. Who in the hell wanted to write a sonnet or a villanelle? We knew what we wanted to write. We wanted to write like the Beat poets, and we knew we wanted to write like Langston Hughes, although he did some form like blues and ballads. But there we were. And I realized from that class that form will not deform you. If I wanted to call myself a poet, it was important that I knew what all these other forms were about.

One time she had us choose a poem to mimic, and I found myself in a bookstore roaming around the poetry section, and I saw this very beautiful book with a flower on it. I sat down on the floor and started to read haiku and I started to cry. It was like I found myself in poems—just like I'd found myself in Langston, but this time I found something else. I found something beyond just the poem. It was the idea of what haiku was all about. It's hard to explain things like this. But there I was. This poem, which was ancient, was also modern. When I began the practice of writing haiku, I realized the form had already been written in my body, in my hand, in my head, before I wrote it down, that it was already in my breath, in my DNA. It was already in my bloodstream.

I understood that through this form of seeking what I call "another truth," I was seeking the truth about what it meant to be Black, and the truth of my people, and my authority as a Black person, and my right to be Black. But there's also the truth of beauty, and that's what I found.

ck: In your articulation of your own ancestral journey, there are curators, and peers, and then, crucially, professors who helped shape your craft. Could you talk about how you work with your own students?

ss: I love teaching, you have no idea. I miss teaching. To go into a classroom, and encounter students who are willing to give their inner thoughts to you—and then engage them in beauty and not anger. They put so much trust in you that you will not destroy them. When I teach I try to be clear that it's not about what is right and what is wrong, but what would work better. So that students know, we don't destroy people in this classroom. We help them to get to better words. We show them how to do that.

CK: We're having this conversation in the middle of the pandemic, still isolating in our homes, and it's hard to hear these reflections on classroom teaching without thinking about the magic of being in the room with other people. You often also talk about the magic that's in a room when you are giving a live reading, standing there invoking beauty. So let's transition from talking about teaching to talking about performing. When you think about your legacy, what is important to you about being on stage in a room with other people?

SS: When I was studying with Bogan, she would take us to hear famous poets read their work. And after she would often say, "He sure can't read, can he?" We wouldn't be sure how to respond, because we were students, and didn't know how far we could go. She would say, "You have to practice. You have to read your work out loud." Because the poem is the dance of the page. When you give it out to an audience, it has got to be there, pulling up, getting ready to soar, dance, spread itself, do the magic that needs to be done, to capture them, to make them enter your arena, and they don't get released until you are at the end of that poem, then you release them. That's the power that you and that poem will have over an audience. You've got to understand that there's music in those lines and in those words. There's magic in them. But there's also authority in there. There's also a responsibility—that is a part of what I teach, the responsibility that you have when you give these words out in an auditorium, in the classroom, to the universe.

I want my students to know that the function of your art is not necessarily to save people from horrors, but to give us all the strength to face them down. And then when the poem is read, it transfers to the audience the responsibility contained in the words.

In my poems I use sound and words that go straight down to our bones, to our guts, to the chains that chained us up, to the leaps off of those boats, to the brutality of when he said, "I can't breathe, I can't breathe, I can't breathe," then you keep holding them on the neck until they really can't breathe anymore. In my early poems, I would write words that would stretch out, I was trying to imitate the sound of a scream, but I would write it out. I was listening to John Coltrane, and all those great musicians, who were playing at that time. I began to imitate their sound, this sound. There was no one who was doing it on page. So therefore we had to figure out how to do it.

But we would call on our ancestors. Who had challenged us to write a scream in a poem that would tell the truth, that would ask for mercy, that would let them see that you come from this herstory and history and you got to tell that story so we can all get to the truth and be whole again.

Sometimes, when we would go see poets, students would say, "I felt like he was acting like a fool on the stage." I would say, "Yeah, he was, wasn't he?" I said. "But when you write what we write, you can never act a fool on a stage. Because your ancestors would be with you always, demanding, challenging you. If you tell the truth, there is no stupidity, there is no foolery."

One of my most powerful ancestral experiences was when I was writing *A Blues Book for Blue Black Magical Women*. I started having these dreams, and I remember the first time I woke up, I was scared. I got up out of the bed. I started coughing. I thought, "Oh my God, you're gonna suffocate." Because I was in this tomb with this woman who was blue—dressed in blue, and she had this blue stuff on her eyelids. And she was comforting me, but I was uncomfortable. I woke up. I woke up and started turning on lights in the bedroom. And I remember I went to the kitchen to put on tea, and I started to write.

Knowing I would have this recurrent dream, I was often hesitant to go to bed. But the woman finally said, "You know you're safe here. I will take care of you." I thought, this is my mother, who'd died giving birth to twins when I was about two years old.

CK: When you dreamt about your mother, what did she have to say? What did she want you to know?

SS: When I dreamt about her while writing *A Blues Book for Blue Black Magical Women*, I was writing a book that I was lost in. But when I began having these dreams with the woman in the tomb, I started asking people what books I should read about Egyptian women. Because I knew this was an Egyptian woman. And I asked historians, also, what books do I read in order to understand what I think I'm experiencing in a dream? About Egyptian women being buried, talking to me about who I am, consoling me about how I was living, opening up to me. So therefore, if you read *A Blues Book for Blue Black Magical Women*, it is a book that is quite different from any other book I've ever written. It is a book that goes back into herstory, and history. It is a book that made me study Egyptian and African themes.

The book has a long epigraph from the Holy Quran and begins with an introduction called "Queens of the Universe," which is about Black women as I knew them. Near the beginning of the second section, called "Past," I write:

because i was born
musician to two
black braids, i
cut a blue song for america.
and you, cushioned
by middleclass springs
saw ghettos
that stretched
voices into dust
turned corners where people
walked on their faces.
I sang unbending
songs and gathered gods
convenient as christ.

It was like I didn't know what I was writing. I would look up after I'd written it and read what I wrote. In the poem "woman" I say:

Come ride my birth, earth mother
tell me how i have become, became
this woman with razor blades between
her teeth.
                sing me my history O earth mother

about tongues multiplying memories
about breaths contained in straw.
pull me from the throat of mankind
where worms eat, O earth mother.
come to this Black woman. you.

. . .

rise up earth mother
out of rope-strung-trees
dancing a windless dance
come phantom mother
dance me a breakfast of births
let your mouth spill me forth
so i creak with your mornings.
come old mother, light up my mind
with a story bright as the sun.

I would go back each night and listen. And I would then get up, go into my study, and look for me in those books. So that's how I wrote that book. The whole book was written always when I looked forward to going to bed and getting the words.

CK: This has been a moving experience. It's been such an honor to talk to you.

SS: Thank you, my sister. I hope you understand the tears. There's some things that you forget, and then you remember. And that was quite an experience for me writing that book.

PROOFREADER
Tyree Daye

Between Duke & Elizabeth is Old Man Dallas,
all three were known as singers & gamblers & cooked
your meat right off the bone.

Near Old Man Dallas's left knee Mr. Brooks,
who carved miniature people out of branches
broken loose by wind & scared the children
because he told them the little men & women had spirits
& Baby Claire swear she saw one move.

At the center Hattie who was building a temple
in her back yard, she had one room of four,
on the door of that room read
bridge to the other side.

Helen was known to see angels
in what old folks called the ether,
& was quoted as saying the church's chimes
seem to say *oh, baby, oh, baby* & ended too soon.
The way *Fire and Desire* ends
& you wish there was a little more.

& there was Miss Bee, who became enchanted
with renaming things she thought had the wrong names.
She would go missing to be found in the wood
holding the rack of a doe saying mama.

I try to stay true to the pronunciation of names
like Buck, Miss Lue, & Uncle C.G. when I go looking for them.

My mama keeps telling me when they call
I don't have to go, but I turn up
like a weed in the collards.

I hold my cellphone flashlight like a ghost lantern.
I steer my body through the dark churchyard,
slow as my mama drove her blue Toyota
down our brown street.

Daye

WOMEN WHO FLY:
NONA HENDRYX AND AFROFUTURIST HISTORIES
Emily Lordi

ON THE LAST NIGHT of Black History Month, February 29, 2020, I attended a concert held in the Temple of Dendur, at New York's Metropolitan Museum of Art—the last such event that I would attend, it turned out, for a very long time. Those who have visited the room will know that it resembles a massive display case: a pavilion-like wall of glass exposes the temple to the sky, and a reflecting pool frames it below. On this night, the temple glowed lavender in the dark behind 600 folding chairs that had been set up to face a makeshift stage. A DJ played songs like Parliament's "Mothership Connection (Star Child)" while four dancers roamed the aisles, voguing and tilting into deep penchés. One dancer, a very tall person with a beard, wore a visored helmet, silver wings, and a skirt made out of a tarp. Before long, a line of people wearing similar costumes and carrying instruments processed up to the stage and started to play—saxophone, synthesizers, arca, drums, bass. A poet, Carl Hancock Rux, recited lyrics about the future. A singer, Keyontia Hawkins, performed incantatory chants.

It was the day before the first case of COVID-19 was confirmed in New York, and several days before the Met would close its doors altogether. But the news was already bad enough that stores were running low on hand soap and it was hard to sit comfortably in a crowd. In this context, the performance felt ominous. Some future was being invoked, and another one receding, but the enigma and the darkness intensified what we always surmise, but seldom admit: there is no telling where we are heading.

Lightly but firmly holding all this sound, dance, and feeling together was Nona Hendryx, the visionary singer best known for her work, in the 1970s, with the women's group Labelle—itself remembered for performing in silver space suits, recording the hit song "Lady Marmalade," and launching the solo career of Patti LaBelle. Hendryx, who is now seventy-six, took a more experimental route than Patti, exploring new genres, technologies, and collaborations with groups such as the Talking Heads and the Black Rock Coalition. Her sheer stamina for sonic innovation across time is matched by very few American artists—George Clinton and Prince, perhaps, as well as the icon to whom her show at the Met was dedicated, Sun Ra.

Ra, who was born in 1914, was a jazz musician, bandleader, and poet who saw ancient Egyptian advances in the arts and sciences as ancestral African inheritances that offered keys to a mythic future. The music he performed with his band, the Arkestra, which he led from the 1950s through the 1990s, was designed to transport listeners to another world. Ra's commitment to myth and space travel—"The sound becomes like a spaceship and lift 'em on out there," he said of his music—has made him a key figure of Afrofuturism. The concept is now used to broadly encompass Black engagements with sci-fi and fantasy, from the 2018 film *Black Panther* to the music of artists whose work, in addition to Ra's, Hendryx was exploring through a year-long residency at Harlem Stage: in the fall of 2019, she staged a tribute to Grace Jones at The Armory, and she had plans to honor George Clinton which were cancelled due to the pandemic. But Hendryx is herself an exemplar of the concept, an artist who embodied Afrofuturist tenets decades before scholars gave them a name.

At the Met, she wore a costume that recalled Sun Ra's aesthetic, as well as mid-1970s Labelle: black helmet, silver headdress, bodysuit, and thigh-high boots. In an alto voice burnished but not weakened by time, she sang esoteric lyrics: "The sky is a sea of darkness when there is no sun to light the way." She was serious, but not overly earnest. "Welcome to the Afrofuturecalifragilistic evening," she said as she greeted the audience. "We are here to honor Sun Ra. More honoring will happen now." Although the museum setting, sacred though it was, threatened to frame Sun Ra as a relic—an artist embraced by those who were lucky enough to have been there, but inaccessible to everyone else—the event nonetheless served as a reminder that there was a there to have witnessed, or missed. Afrofuturism, that is, despite its status as a perennial cutting-edge pop culture trend, has a history and a trajectory. It has a gender. And it has ancestors who come not only from ancient Egypt but from places as local as New Jersey, who are still with us.

THESE DAYS, the word Afrofuturism serves as a catchall for work across artistic and diasporic spectrums—the fiction of Samuel R. Delany and

N.K. Jemisin, the visual art of Wangechi Mutu, the music of Janelle Monáe, the films of John Akomfrah. But the term, which was coined by scholar Mark Dery in 1994, arose in response to quite specific conversations about the *near* future. Discussions of cyberculture in the nineties often marginalized people of color and treated race as a liability. Whether theorists celebrated cyberspace as an "escape" from racial identity or worried that race-based hierarchies would only deepen due to the "digital divide" (unequal distribution of access and skills), both camps, scholar Alondra Nelson pointed out in 2002, shared "the assumption that race . . . in the twenty-first century is either negligible or evidence of negligence." Afrofuturism was, in Nelson's terms, an alternative "critical perspective" that acknowledged, without necessarily lamenting, the difference that race could make—in cyberspace, and in the history of science and technology generally.

That critical lens helped scholars to expose and reframe the work of Black inventors—to see a figure such as Madame C. J. Walker, for instance, not only as a haircare guru but as a chemist. The Afrofuturist paradigm also revealed how Black speculative fiction challenged white sci-fi and fantasy worlds in which Black characters were absent, demonized, or among the first to die. And it showed how Black life under modernity had been "sci-fi" from the beginning. If, as scholar Tricia Rose argued, chattel slavery had made Black people the first robots—human figures forced to serve other humans—it had also made Black life in the United States surreal and fantastic. Slave narratives bear this out. What could be more sci-fi, writer Greg Tate recently asked me, than an enslaved man, Henry "Box" Brown, literally mailing himself to freedom?

Lordi

Nearly twenty years after Nelson's landmark assessment, Afrofuturism has become not only an analytical framework but a cultural current with powerful emotional reach. It gives self-described Black nerds a sense of community, and provides others with a non-fatalistic vision of Black identity—one "rooted in the past," Nelson writes, "but not weighed down by it." Literary historian Britt Rusert recently told me, "Afrofuturism, today, has come to be increasingly inflected by the sentiments of the Black Lives Matter movement and the 'radical' idea that Black people deserve to exist and thrive in the future."

Still, discussions of Afrofuturism often privilege male figures. Even those who recognize Black women's presence in the tradition tend to downplay their leadership of it. (A recent article by Jonita Davis bucks this trend, as does a chapter in Ytasha L. Womack's 2013 book *Afrofuturism: The World of Black Sci-Fi and Fantasy Culture*.) Female Afrofuturists are generally framed as exceptions to male rule (June Tyson's role as a vocalist with Sun Ra's all-male Arkestra) or as accessories to male power (the Brides of Funkenstein who performed with Funkadelic). But Black women have not only worn the space-age costumes, they have designed them; have not only sung the songs but produced them. Put metaphorically: they have been riding the Mothership, but they have also been manning it. Hendryx's career embodies this principle. To make this point is to write her into a Black male–dominated narrative of Afrofuturist innovation just as insistently as scholars such as Maureen Mahon and Sonnet Retman have written her into (or into productive tension with) a rock genealogy presumed to be the domain of white men. Who better to ask about her early and ongoing work with Afrofuturism, I figured, than Hendryx herself?

THE DAY AFTER her Sun Ra tribute, I met with her at the Redeye Grill in midtown Manhattan. Looking tired yet stylish in a tailored jacket and scarf, she explained that her first love was not music but science. Growing up in Trenton, New Jersey, in the 1940s and '50s, she was obsessed with astronomy, space travel, and what was then called not "technology" but "electronics." She watched her brother fix cars, and sat mesmerized as cartoon space ships floated across her TV screen. "Music was not the object of my desire," she said. "It was not anywhere in the realm of my thinking." But her friend Sarah Dash invited her to join a singing group, and before long, the group, the Bluebells—Dash, Hendryx, Cindy Birdsong, and Patricia Holt (later Patti LaBelle)—had a manager and a Top 10 hit.

Even as Hendryx's career in music took off, she continued to dream of the future and outer space. While on tour, she read Superman comics and watched late-night cult movies like *Attack of the 50 Foot Woman* (1958). She loved singing with the women in Labelle, who were like her sisters. But what sustained her life in music was the art and science of recording. She wrote poems, which became songs, and learned how to use technology to translate her musical ideas into sound. "That's when I thought—oh, *this* is amazing." She studied every aspect of the process, from the synthesizers and sequencers to "the oxidation of tape, and how air is compressed—how you get the sound of my voice onto tape."

These skills and interests were not expected of women in the industry. "You were told to look pretty and sing," Hendryx said. "It was a man's world. The business was run by men." There were some women who ran labels and played instruments, but the rules of engagement were limited: as a woman, "you could write songs, you could sing the songs, you could front the songs, but it was really—it was Phil Spector, it was Bob Crewe, it was the *guys* who made the music. They had the labels, they were the people in charge. The fashion, even the makeup, was male-dominated. Women were secretaries."

But the late sixties—an era that sent astronauts to the moon and everyday people to Vietnam—was a catalytic moment for tech-minded artists with dreams of better lives and other worlds. At a certain point, Hendryx explained, the zeitgeist seemed to be on her side. The British Invasion, "the sex, drugs, and rock 'n' roll–flower power mixture," and the innovations of producers like John Cage and Suzanne Ciani forced a reckoning: "Either as an artist you were willing to change, or you were going to become a sort of caricature of what you were in the sixties—you know, a girl group still wearing gowns, still wearing wigs and gloves and singing." Labelle connected with artists in Europe and on the West Coast, and drew inspiration from women like Grace Slick, Chaka Khan, and Betty Davis (the latter was a kindred spirit, not only because of her "huge Afro and African Space aesthetic," but because she led her own band). So began the group's voyage into glam rock iconicity.

Larry LeGaspi, a Puerto Rican designer and Labelle groupie, had a shop in the West Village called Moonstone that "was a moonscape," Hendryx recalled, filled with black and silver "moon rocks and things we imagine as the moon." LeGaspi started to make space-themed costumes for Labelle (taking over the role from Hendryx herself). Meanwhile, Hendryx wrote songs about the future: "Cosmic

Dancer," "Space Children," "A Man in a Trench Coat (Voodoo)." Before long, "Lady Marmalade" topped both R&B and pop charts, and Labelle became the first Black female group to appear on the cover of *Rolling Stone*. Their visual and sonic evolution culminated in 1975 with their legendary "wear something silver" concert at the Metropolitan Opera House. People came as "nuns dressed in silver, horses and carriages, and Salvador Dalí. Just the really insane people of New York came to the Met," Hendryx said. "That was the real crux of the Afrofuturism movement."

Now, forty-some years later, Afrofuturism has reemerged, having picked up a name and new meanings. But Hendryx resists the idea of a renaissance in favor of continuity. Afrofuturism has "always been there," she said. "There's a whole group of speculative fiction nerd people, of which I count myself one," who connect online and eventually collaborate—"you sort of come out of your Afrofuturism closet at some point and go 'Ah, yes, I am just a nerd as well! I may look like this,'" she said, gesturing at her glamorous self, "'but this is what I am.'"

For the past decade, she has turned a great deal of her collaborative energy toward education. In the Berklee College of Music's Electronic Production and Design Department, she nurtures students' (especially young women's) interest in sound recording. And she has founded a high school mentoring program, SistersMATR (Math, Art, Technology, and Robotics), to encourage girls of color in STEM fields. Insofar as her pedagogical and creative roles intersect, the stage itself is a laboratory for her. Realizing this, I came to see that the point of the Sun Ra show had not been to christen the audience with Sun Ra's cosmic vibrations, but to demonstrate a historical principle:

that Black women have long been authors and architects of science and myth. Both online and in real life, they have built the kinds of networks of which cyberspace optimists dreamed—but they have done so while cherishing the identities that those enthusiasts denied.

Toward the end of our conversation, Hendryx waxed oracular on networks, quantum theory, and the interpenetration of all things. The subject of COVID-19 came up, as was inevitable: New York's first case would be breaking news mere hours after our lunch date. "The scientists that are looking at the virus now," Hendryx said, "they know there is no separation between us and it. And it is far more powerful than we are. . . . And it is constantly mutating as it's evolving. We just evolve so much slower because we are a larger virus than it is." She wasn't afraid, she said, because "there's no such thing as the future."

"There's no such thing as the future," I repeated dumbly, a writer whose entire subject seemed to be on the verge of unraveling. "No," she said. "There is always now. I can't be anywhere else but now. Which is fantastic, because it's everything. And whatever the next second is, that is that. And whatever the last second is, is really of no consequence. So there's nothing to be afraid of, because, I can *say* that that was that, and I can *surmise* that that's going be that. But what I *do* know is this moment."

To extend this theory to Hendryx's music is to realize that its purpose is less to launch us into imagined elsewheres than to embed us more deeply into the exclusively knowable now. Nonetheless, her musical tributes, to figures like Sun Ra and Grace Jones, also maintain the importance of history. Quantum theory might challenge conventional notions of time, but *history*, the way the past gets told, remains as important as ever. "I didn't learn about Black history," Hendryx noted on a livestream panel held in October in tribute to Little Richard. "When you don't learn about your history . . . you don't push that history forward." History teaches us, for one, that Black women artists, thinkers, and activists have long been perfecting techniques for propelling themselves and others beyond an impossible present. What else do you call the grassroots activism Stacey Abrams performed to flip the state of Georgia from red to blue in the 2020 presidential and Senate elections? This is what it is to be told *by some* that the future is not for you—and to go about making one anyway, be it fantastic or blessedly mundane.

"Now we're finding out about all these 'hidden figures'," Hendryx told me. "Katherine Johnson, who just died—she was one of *my* heroes, who *I* knew about, but nobody else knew about these women." It matters when Hollywood represents such women in films such as *Hidden Figures* (2016), and when the culture at large grants them, however belatedly, recognition and respect. It might matter especially to Black women themselves, who still need to find each other, and who have sometimes been the *only* ones pushing each other into their own eccentric futures. Hendryx spoke about African American astronaut Mae Jemison, an idol of hers who has since become a friend. "She did what I wanted to do," Hendryx said. "And I met her, and I was like, 'Oh my God, you fulfilled my dream.' And she said, 'Well, the song I listened to as I prepared for my travel into space was your song, "Women Who Fly." That was my inspiration.'"

NIGHT PICNIC

Izumi Suzuki, translated from the Japanese
by Sam Bett

JUNIOR'S DAD CAME IN while he was studying at his desk. "Well? How's it coming along?" Dad looked over Junior's shoulder, mouthing a cigarette.

"Good . . . Hey, aren't you supposed to light those things?"

"Oh, right. I keep forgetting."

Dad produced a lighter from his pocket and lit the cigarette. He drew the smoke into his lungs.

"Come on, Dad. You're the one who's always saying that we can't forget to act like Earthlings."

"Got me there. Sorry, son . . . I know it's up to me to set a good example for the family. As Earthlings, it's our responsibility, regardless of the time or place, to carry on our way of life. To be the very model of a family. Especially since we're so far away from Earth, out here on our own."

"Yeah. I guess you're right." He examined his father's outfit. Dad wore a black double-breasted suit, paired with a black shirt and a white tie. Red rose thrust in the buttonhole of his lapel, hat on his head, thick rings cladding his fingers.

"Spiffy, huh? Pretty sharp for your old dad. I took a couple of cues from a guy I saw on a video I was watching earlier, all dressed up and dancing."

"Hey, I watched that one too. So I guess that makes this a dancing costume?" Junior weighed his words, careful not to sound like he was talking back.

"Ridiculous." Dad puffed out his chest. "In other videos, I've seen guys wear this kind of thing while riding in cars, or having their nails trimmed at the barber shop. And everyone who sees them treats them with respect. Which, if you ask me, makes this the perfect outfit for a father."

"OK, but how come you're almost twice as fat as yesterday?"

"You have to be this big, or else a double-breasted suit won't look right," Dad ventured, lacking conviction.

Junior decided not to argue. He shut his book. "I'm making decent progress with deciphering for the day. Honestly, now that I've got the hang of it . . . It's kinda fun."

"No one's forcing you to enjoy it . . . I wonder if this book's legit, though. Seems there are three kinds of books: ones that are all lies, ones that are half lies and half true, and ones that are true through and through. Hard telling which is which."

"You got that right. Why is that? Why bother stringing all those words together if the end result is one big lie?"

Father and son pondered the question. This was a persistent mystery to them. Junior in particular was skeptical. They assumed the videos, at least, were telling the truth, but what were they supposed to do if those were lying, too?

"We human beings are complicated creatures." Dad sighed. This observation, while not exactly helpful, struck him as a pretty cool thing to say.

"I think this book is true, though," Junior said. "It even provides a date for everything."

"Righto! Keen observation, boy. So smart. Like a father, like a son." Dad beamed. "You know, I failed to notice that myself. It's hard to tell what aeon most of these books come from."

"This one's set in nineteenth-century America. I found it on the map. It talks about the War Between the States. But the main character's a woman."

"Once you're finished deciphering, tell me if they explain why humans ventured into space."

"I'm not so sure they will, but I'll keep going anyway. This woman just had her heart broken. Look how many pages I still have left though! So maybe there's time yet for her to wind up on a spaceship. I mean, when people get jilted, don't they usually skip town?" The gifted son spoke with certainty.

"Suppose so . . ." Dad cocked his head.

"You know, like take a trip? You hear a lot of that in songs."

"I guess so."

"I kinda want to try getting my heart broken."

"I think you'd need to be in a relationship . . ."

"What about my sister?"

"Right. Sure, worth a try."

"First, though, we have to meet up at a dance party, or go on a date or something."

"Don't get your hopes up. There's only four of us Earthlings left, after all . . . Who else would you invite? The monsters that gambol they beyond the hill they do?"

"Wait, but can't those guys transform so that they look exactly like us? We could make them tons of nice clothes with the replicator. Then they'd have something to wear."

"They don't have any interest in that kind of thing. The concept of a civilized existence is beyond them. We're lucky they're tame. They won't do us any harm, but they're obviously a different form of life. Who knows what they're thinking? They'd have a lot more fun if they were living in our automated city. But they insist on roughing it. They must prefer it that way."

Mom poked her head into the room, hair knobbed with curlers. "You need to talk some sense into that girl . . ." She wore a bathrobe and held an orange and a glass of milk.

"What's wrong?" asked Dad.

"She's hiding in the closet again."

"Huh? What's bothering her this time?"

"It's these awful books. Now she's started reading about how daughters hate their moms and love their dads. As if I needed this today." Mom shook her head.

"What?" Dad asked, perplexed. "What's she been reading?"

"*Psychology* or something. What a load of baloney."

Junior assumed a noble air. "Don't worry, I'll get her out."

"Let me do it," Dad insisted. "I call the shots around here, see."

Suzuki

"Yeah, but Dad, what do you know about books?" Junior left the room.

"HOW LONG ARE YOU GOING to keep this up? Get out of there right now!" Mom pounded on the door.

"Go away!" said Sis. "I'm being rebellious."

The response was muffled, as if her face was buried in a cushion.

"You've got it wrong, Sis," Junior said.

"How so?" she asked. "I'm an adolescent."

"We're supposed to be going on a picnic!" Mom shrieked.

"Get out this instant!"

"Hush a minute, will you?" Junior pushed Mom aside, but pushed too hard. She tumbled to the floor and bashed her forehead. For a while she lay still. Leaving her like that, Junior crossed his arms.

"Were you reading about the Electra Complex?"

"Yeah," Sis answered from the closet.

"Did you know that there's a negative Oedipus Complex, too, though?"

"Huh?" Her voice was quiet. "What's that?"

"It's when you form an attachment to a parent of the same sex."

". . . Isn't that the opposite?"

"Exactly. In psychology, for any given case, there's generally another case that constitutes the polar opposite. Though not in every single situation."

". . . Really?" Sis was losing confidence in her position.

"I've read more books than any of us, right?"

No response.

Mom sat up, feeling woozy. She rubbed her forehead for a while. Apparently it wasn't serious. She went over to the replicator.

"Besides, do you realize how bored you're gonna get if you stay cooped up in the closet?" Junior was changing strategies.

". . . But . . ."

"You call yourself an adolescent, but that's bogus. This place has a different orbital period than Earth. Not like I've actually done the math, but I bet they're different alright." Junior tried to sound as nonchalant as possible.

"How old are you again?" he asked. "In local years."

"Um, I guess . . . like seventeen or something?" Sis was earnest, but sounded doubtful. "I'm not sure though. Sometimes my calendar stops working."

"Know what you mean. After a week, it's all a blur. I've been trying to pinpoint when it was that human beings invented time. I'm still trying to figure it out, but evidently time was a big deal."

Junior pulled up a chair and sat. In imitation of his father, he had a smoke. When he ashed on the floor, the robovacuum scurried over.

"Yeah, but that's exactly why I'm doing this." Sis fidgeted in the closet.

"Don't you realize?" Junior asked. "Time is bogus. After 3 p.m. today, for all we know it'll be 7 a.m. four days ago."

Mom craned her neck at Junior. She was in the process of pulling a bamboo basket from the replicator. "What are you saying? Time is passing just fine, thank you very much. We're the ones who need to make sure that we keep on acting normally. Now get your sister

Suzuki

out of the closet. Once I've got everything together, we're heading out. This has been on the docket for quite a while."

"I get it, OK?"

Junior turned around, knitting his brow. Sometimes, it was OK to get upset with your parents. It was a regular occurrence in the dramas on TV.

"Let's talk about time later. Seventeen, huh? That's pretty old to be going through adolescence."

". . . So, what am I supposed to do?" she asked reluctantly.

"Well, women in their late teens wash their hair excessively. They stand in front of the mirror, trying on tons of different clothes. Sometimes they go on dates."

"Is that supposed to be more fun?"

"Yeah, absolutely. Tons of fun."

"Alright."

The door slid open from inside. Sis was sitting in the top compartment of the closet, hugging a pillow. Nimbly, she jumped down to the floor.

"Whew, I'm tired. I was in there six whole hours. Mom took forever to notice." She reached both arms up and stretched.

"We were busy, that's all," said Junior, attempting to console her.

"I try to be rebellious, and our folks don't even notice." Just like that, her voice was buoyant.

Mom headed for the kitchen, arms full of picnic fixings.

"What's that woman doing?" asked Sis.

"Making us lunch. And it's a little weird to call your mom 'that woman'."

"It's fine once in a while."

"If you say so." Junior didn't really know himself.

"I'm going to get ready," Sis said.

His little sister stood before the replicator and punched a series of buttons.

"INSUFFICIENT VEGETABLE OIL," quoth the replicator. Among the contents of the basket Mom had set beside the machine was a tub of margarine. Sis scraped the tub clean with a knife, emptying it into the hopper. The processing light flickered. At length, two tubes of lipstick popped from the machine, accompanied by a gentle tone.

"Hey, think it can make some stuff for me?"

"Sure."

"Let's see . . . I'll need a comb and some pomade. Or maybe gel instead."

"Changing your hairstyle?"

"Yeah. Can't decide if I'm gonna spike it up or do a pompadour."

Junior thought of all the coming-of-age movies he had seen. All the different styles showcased in the bromides. Granted, the movies had a tendency to overrepresent the *American Graffiti* look.

"I'll have some pomade."

"What make?" Sis shot back.

He hadn't thought of that. "Do I gotta be specific?"

"The devil is in the details. If you care anything about fashion." Sis was a stickler for minutiae.

"What kinds are there? I don't know where to start."

"So for your different brands of product . . . there's Yanagiya, Fiorucci, Lanvin . . ." Sis was showing off.

"That many kinds?"

"Then there's Nestlé, Ajinomoto, Kewpie . . ."

"Gimme one of the good ones." Sis manipulated the machine and pulled out a jar of pomade. It had a Kewpie emblem on the lid.

"It's the little things in life that matter."

"So I hear."

"I know way more about this kind of thing than you. I read the women's magazines. I even know more about Sunday brunch than Mom. Girls are supposed to eat yogurt and fruit. Oh, and cheesecake."

"Look at you, acting like a real girl now." Junior was genuinely impressed. "Correct me if I'm wrong, but didn't you used to be a boy?"

"Think so. It's all kind of vague. Mom and Dad decided that having one boy and one girl would make for more variety. But the hairstyle and clothes are totally different. It's a real pain. If I was still a boy, I could just copy you."

Junior thought back to when his sister was a boy. They both wore shorts and chased each other around, playing tag. Mom was adamant that a child with a girlish body should be raised to be a woman. So his little brother became a little sister. Sis seemed fine with it. After dressing as a girl for a while, her body was much softer looking than before. Thanks to no small effort on her part.

"Where's Mom?" Nothing else to do, Junior paced around the room.

"Isn't she getting dressed?"

"What's taking her so long?"

"Hellooo! When women go out, it takes them a long time to get ready."

"But all she has to do is change her clothes, comb her hair, and put on a little makeup."

"That's not the point . . ."

"Well, what else is there?"

"I dunno . . . but moms have a lot of stuff to do, like all the time. Families depend on every member acting out their roles."

Junior went back to his room. He lay down on his bed and put on a tape. Pretty soon, he nodded off.

It took Mom two and a half days to get ready. The four of them left the house carrying baskets and thermoses. What a clear, gorgeous night it was.

"Aren't we driving?"

"Then it wouldn't be a picnic, dummy."

They strolled along, buildings towering on either side. It would appear this city had no residents but them. The windows shone a secretive blue. The buildings were dark inside, cloaked in quietude. Far off in the distance, a steady humming could be heard. Automated switches flicking on and off. Following the curving road, the mercury lamps looked like a string of race cars.

"The view is awful over here," Dad whispered.

"Don't people usually go on picnics to enjoy the scenery?" Sis asked her brother.

"They go to fields and hills and stuff. Places with big trees."

"But isn't it unsafe to leave the city?"

Mom turned, eyeing them anxiously. Not a single one of them had any memory of being outside the city, but somehow, they shared an understanding of what the world outside the city looked like. It ended

Suzuki

abruptly. Rather than a gradual thinning of the buildings, there was a stark line at the edge, as if the whole metropolis had been sliced out from somewhere else and plopped down on this planet. Like the family, it came across as woefully isolated. They had no idea when this city came to be. Settlers from Earth had built this settlement, and for one reason or another fled or all but died out, leaving the few perseverant souls from whom they were descended. At least, as Dad would have it. Outside the city, hills and fields stretched off into the distance, where prowled the blue-black monsters. Thick bristles on their crowns and backs, squat-legged creatures they. Trotting about on their hindlegs. Their front legs were brawny; black claws grew from their fingertips. They appeared to be indifferent to the presence of this Earthling clan.

Though none of them had ever seen one of the monsters, they knew how they looked and behaved. Inexplicably. The monsters subsisted on tree nuts and were exceedingly benign. Or perhaps not benign, Dad told them once, so much as indolent. It was unclear whether they were napping or slacking off. Hence, they could not be human. Human beings, he said, were supposed to lead orderly lives. Their family being a prime example.

"Dad," asked Mom, "did you read the morning paper?"

"Yeah," Dad answered solemnly. He was the one who had insisted they read the newspaper, to "keep up with the Joneses."

A person who neglects to read the news each morning is a bum, like those who fail to pay their cable bill. But then again, they only used the TV to watch tapes. So who cares about the cable bill. It's not like there were any stations anyway. The newspaper, however, was indispensable. The fact that there was no newspaper company was no excuse.

Using articles from magazines and old newspapers, Dad made his own gazette. Each night before bed, he pushed the shuffle button. If he was too punctilious with the selection, it would spoil the surprise. And he made sure he set the postometer accordingly, so that the paper landed in the mailbox at 5 a.m. each morning.

"Anything good?" Mom had no interest in the news but let on like she cared.

"Price of wheat's gone up."

"Again? That's the sixth time this month." Her response was artificial, and why not? The articles were artificial too. All that mattered was that they went through the motions.

"It plateaued for a while, though." Dad was being difficult. "Look, I've been giving it some thought." He crossed his arms and watched their son and daughter, who were now a little ways ahead. "I think it's time we built a house."

"Why is that? What's wrong with where we're living now?"

"We can't stay there forever. The only plus about that place is that we're settled in. It's been too long already. We need to resist the temptation of perpetual convenience, every corner spic and span. Human beings only grow through hardship. Building a house is a man's life's work."

"Where will we go?" Mom figured why not ask. She knew it was ridiculous, but when he got like this, she had to do her best to play along.

"Where? That's why we're here . . . to find the perfect spot." She wouldn't dream of living outside the city. Besides, Dad had no clue how to build a house.

"I will avoid a casual approach to life at any cost." But Dad immediately qualified himself, to smooth things over. "I simply don't want us to wind up the butt of the joke. When people behave shamefully, their children follow suit. Children only notice when their parents make mistakes. One false move, and pretty soon they're . . . You know, whatever you call it." Dad flapped his hand impatiently.

"Delinquents?"

"Right, right. In no time flat. Who knows why, but kids love being delinquent." He was emphatic, though not exactly sure what being a delinquent entailed. It sounded like something from the newspaper, but then again, he was the newspaper.

"I blame it on the motorcycles."

"Damn straight. Great point, Mom. That's the problem. Motorcycles and cars!"

"But they already have both. They made them with the replicator."

"Hmm, I don't like the sound of this. We'll have to figure out a subtle way of talking sense into them. Discipline is all about taking the right approach." They continued down the deserted street.

"How much further?"

Junior produced his comb and ran it through his hair, making a ducktail at the back of his neck. He took care to ensure that the hair met in a vertical line. A solitary bang fell across his forehead. *I got this,* he told himself. *I am the coolest cat.* Sis wore an evening gown with a lengthy train. The proper attire for going out at night. She knew the deal. She had debated wearing something disco-formal, but it's not like they were going to a disco, so she gave up on that idea. Someday, though, she hoped to see a disco, at least once, but Dad refused to let her go. He called them dens of ill repute. Thanks to him, she never got to go where all the groovy kids were at. Wherever that was.

"Hey, we're not leaving town, are we?" asked Sis.

"Uh, actually, I think we are," said Junior. He popped the collar of his button-down shirt, just for show. Maybe he should untuck the front.

"I wish there were an ocean nearby. Seaside highways are so dreamy." She was thinking of a scene from one of the videos.

They arrived at a plaza, theaters on all sides. Fountain in the middle. All the lights were out.

"Hey, what happened here? It's usually so spectacular."

"Late at night, they turn the lights off."

"What time you think it is?"

"Hard to say," said Junior. "Besides, clocks are bogus. I even get the feeling that time flows differently depending on what part of the city you're in." He stuffed his hands into his pockets.

"We left early in the evening, though. And we haven't walked for very long."

"Now that you mention it, yeah."

Lately, he'd been losing confidence in how to live his life. Some days he had no idea what to do with himself. Especially when time started expanding and contracting. That really screwed him up. Seeing the sun go down while he was still working on his morning coffee was deeply upsetting. If he sat up doing nothing all hours of the night, his parents scolded him, saying nighttime was for sleeping. When he said he wasn't sleepy, they told him to pretend. Anything else would be indecent. He wasn't to be doing anything disgraceful to society. He had no idea what they meant by "society." What were they referring to? If he asked, his parents screamed, "You've got no common sense! At your age, shouldn't you have some common sense already?" So he waited for his common sense to arrive on its own. He'd been waiting for a while now. No sign of it anywhere.

Junior worried all the time. (Books told him growing up was about agony and doubt. So maybe this was how it was supposed to be.) He sat down beside his sister.

"Hey, do you think time is made up?" Sis looked at him.

"Anywhere there's no people," he said, "there's no such thing as time. It's something people made up, out of convenience. To impose order on events."

"What about history? We're trying to find out what really happened. When and how human beings made it here. Don't you want to know what it was like when they first arrived?"

"These days, I'm not sure I really care about that anymore. Feels immaterial."

"Watch what you're thinking, boy." Dad called to him from the bench where he sat.

"Enough. Quit jabbering." He shook his head. "You've got it all wrong, son. Why do you think we read books and watch videos? To learn about the way of life of those who came before us. That's why. They offer us a clear example of how to live life right. We must keep on the straight and narrow. If we go astray, we're toasted."

"I think each person should live life how they like."

"That's immaturity for you. At your age, you should be going to school, getting drowned in homework. You should be thankful for being spared that fate . . . Though life would be a whole lot easier for me if there were a school around here. And for you too. On Earth, they had something called entrance exams."

"I know."

"It would do you good to have an outlet for your youthful vigor. Burning your glory days on tests—ah, that takes me back!" Dad spread his arms theatrically. "That's what being young is all about! Testing your mettle. The satisfaction of giving it your all. The beauty!"

"You want me to be some kind of clean-cut poster boy?"

"What else is youth good for?"

"No thanks. Sounds pretty lame. Lately, I've been doubting the advisability of giving anything your all."

"I'm saying this for your own good, son. Your folks would not mislead you. So listen up."

"Is that why you're having me create a history of Earthlings, in place of sending me to school? Why do you care so much about history and time, anyway?"

"Have you gone rotten, boy? So, you think you can get away with being a delinquent, huh? Bad kids always spout the same blatherskite."

"Listen to your father. You'll regret this one of these days. It's like the saying goes: there's no use holding a village at the family grave. Once we're dead, it'll be too late."

"Don't you mean *vigil*?"

"Same difference. You little brat."

Junior shut his mouth. He understood the problem, however tenuously. His parents were uncomfortable with playing Earthlings on this foreign planet. In an effort to conceal their discomfort, they obsessively adhered to social customs, codes of behavior. Since they were unsure of what, exactly, was the best way for an Earthling to behave, they held themselves and their children to impossible ideals. Their pursuit of the history of their ancestors, too, was a function of their desire for peace of mind.

"Are you a bad boy now?" asked Sis. "Just a few days ago, weren't you a goody two-shoes?" She asked this sincerely (not as an accusation).

"That's right. I find it pretty odd myself. While Mom was getting ready to go out, I started thinking about time. After two and a half days of thinking, I realized the idea of linear time does no one any good. If all that matters is survival."

"I only took an hour. Is your head screwed on OK?" Mom, who was wearing a neckerchief for the excursion, shook her head with vigor.

This got Junior thinking. What if I'm the only one unstuck from time?

"Hold on, dear. I think that's going too far."

"You're probably right. I only want our children to be safe. Sometimes I get carried away . . ."

Mom giggled, covering her mouth with her hand. Then she looked up at her family and gave them a command, in a voice honeyed with enthusiasm. "Forget I said anything. Let's eat."

The monsters were huddled together, flank to flank, asleep. The cushy undergrowth provided matchless bedding. A sweet smell wafted from the earth, but the sensual aroma of the trees was overpowering. The beasts were fast asleep, without a care. Except for two. Eyes open to the night, they pondered time and the liberty of other living things.

The Earthling family chomped their sandwiches in silence. Before they swallowed their first bites, dawn visited the planet.

"Hey, what's going on? This can't be."

"What did I tell you? Don't forget to bring your watch," Mom said. "Who knows what ungodly hour we left the house." She nudged Dad with her elbow.

"This can't be happening." Dad's jaw fell open.

"Can't? It's happening, alright, clear as day. What now?"

"I don't see why we can't picnic during the day," said Sis. She ate her sandwich beatifically.

"Don't point fingers at me," Mom snapped. "Your father's the one who picked the time."

"I wanted it to be like in that movie, *Picnic on the Night*." Dad hadn't a leg to stand on.

"Isn't it *Picnic on the Battlefield*?" Junior interjected.

"Don't talk back, you little shit!" Mom said. "If we wanted to do that, we'd have to march off into a warzone! Do you realize how hard it is to find a proper battle in this day and age? Of course you don't. Because you don't know anything. You're confused." Mom was borderline hysterical.

"Isn't there a *Picnic on Nearside*, too?" Sis looked at the faces of her family members. None of them seemed to know what she was talking about.

"Oh well. Let's go home." Dad spoke with much chagrin. They took their leave.

Something scurried by and stole their picnic basket. A girl. She glanced back at them from the entrance to a theater. Fulgurous eyes and hair of gold had she.

"Hey, what gives!" Dad yelled. "That's ours."

"My cutwork napkins are in there!" Mom cried. "Don't let her get away with that."

Suzuki

The girl slung the basket over her shoulder and darted off. She was fast. The family pursued.

"Dad gave me those for our anniversary, in a set with the table-cloth. They're priceless." Mom wailed as she ran.

Just when they thought they'd lost her, they saw the girl at the next intersection, waiting for them on the corner.

"She not an Earthling be! I'm positive that we're the only actual Earthlings left!" Dad was out of steam.

"Are there unactual Earthlings? What would that involve?"

"Quiet! This is no time for insubordination."

"Can't you make more napkins with the replicator?" asked Sis, keeping pace.

"They have sentimental value! They're the only ones in the entire universe!" Mom was blowing things out of proportion.

This game of tag—running full speed and stopping short, then dashing off again—continued for some time.

"If she's hungry, we would've shared, but this is unforgivable."

"I bet she's trying to lure us off somewhere."

In which case, you would think they would've given up on chasing her, but the parents ran like mad. Junior and Sis chased the girl, too, though not without a modicum of glee. They reached the edge of the city. The girl atop a gentle hill stood she.

"No one makes a fool outta this family. We'll get you yet!"

"Stop, dear, it's too dangerous."

The four of them stood their ground, eyes trained on the hilltop. An elder appeared from the shade of a great tree and stood behind the girl.

"Sorry for your trouble. I hoped to speak with you, but our kind, as a rule, cannot enter the city. Not because we are unable to, but because we hate it there. It's made by human beings for human beings. No place for us." The elder's speech was stilted, though his voice was soft.

"Give it back!" Mom was frantic.

"When we are finished, I will return your things. Long we have been watching you. Not with our eyes, but with our minds. Since this is something that you're capable of too, I think you'll understand?"

"We have no clue who you are!" Dad was flushed with anger.

"Please, hear me out. Once upon a time, we lived in peace. We may not have manufactured or consumed, but our existences were rich. Alas, in any group, there will always be misfits. Some of us began to wonder why they were alive and where they came from. Their thoughts consumed their every moment. Eventually they set off for the city. The city made by denizens of another star, and then abandoned. Once there, they spent their days deliberating about time and history and origins." The elder didn't sound the least bit elderly.

"Are you talking about us? Well, you can quit while you're ahead. We're not like you. We were born in this city. Lived here our whole lives!" Dad was livid.

"So you don't remember. The memory, however, has a tendency to reorganize itself rather conveniently. I figured it was time to set you straight. Which is why we've led you here. Why do you insist on roleplaying as Earthlings—or whatever riffraff you purport to be? You can be free, without such pageantries of humankind. A calm existence, unplagued by these anxieties, is within reach."

Suzuki

"Asshole!"

Dad swelled with malice. His body literally swelled. Violent shockwaves daggered from his person. Foul electricity, filthy purple. The waves crested the hill and zapped the elder and the girl, killing them instantly. The family had no idea what was going on. They had never suspected their rising tempers could physically kill someone.

"Phew!" Mom pointed. "Not human after all." Two blue-black monsters slumped at the top of the hill.

"Man, what a surprise!" Junior snickered. When he beheld the faces of his family, he saw three monsters.

A breeze swept the tranquil hillside. The monsters who had posed as a family stood stock still, overtaken with amazement.

They could not wrap their heads around what had transpired or why. Feeling stupid, they remembered now that monsters (such as them) were able to take any form. Perhaps they had been so convinced they were Earthlings that they began to look the part.

The wind changed.

Disregarding one another, the monsters loped off, each heading its own way. Leisurely, with no particular place to go, stewards of a new anxiety.

CONTRIBUTORS

Bennet Bergman is founding editor of *Changes*. His poems have appeared in *Three-penny Review* and *Gulf Coast*.

Sam Bett was awarded Grand Prize in the 2016 JLPP International Translation Competition and won the 2019/2020 Japan–U.S. Friendship Commission Prize for his translation of *Star* by Yukio Mishima.

Tyree Daye is Teaching Assistant Professor at UNC-Chapel Hill. He is author of *River Hymns*, winner of the 2017 APR/Honickman First Book Prize, and *Cardinal*.

Diamond Forde is author of *Mother Body* and winner of the Pink Poetry Prize, the Furious Flower Poetry Prize, and CLA's Margaret Walker Memorial Prize. Her work has appeared in *Massachusetts Review*, *Ninth Letter*, *NELLE*, and *Tupelo Quarterly*.

Duana Fullwiley is author of *The Enculturated Gene: Sickle Cell Health Politics and Biological Difference in West Africa* as well as numerous articles on ancestry genetics in the United States. She is Associate Professor of Anthropology at Stanford University.

José B. González is author of *Toys Made of Rock* and *When Love Was Reels*, and is editor of LatinoStories.com.

Racquel Goodison is faculty at the City University of New York. Her writing has appeard in the *Obsidian*, *Pleiades*, *Your Impossible Voice*, *Kweli Journal*, *Her Kind*, and *Drunken Boat*. Her chapbook *Skin* was a finalist for the 2013 Goldline Press Fiction Chapbook Prize and winner of the 2013–14 Creative Justice Press Fiction Chapbook Prize.

Terrance Hayes is a MacArthur Fellow and author, most recently, of *American Sonnets for My Past And Future Assassin* and *To Float In The Space Between: Drawings and Essays in Conversation with Etheridge Knight*. He won the National Book Award for *Lighthead*.

Day Heisinger-Nixon holds an MA in Deaf Studies from Gallaudet University and has been published in *Apogee Journal*, *Foglifter*, and *Booth*. They live in Los Angeles.

Tyehimba Jess is author of *leadbelly* and *Olio*, for which he won the Pulitzer Prize for Poetry. He is Professor of English at College of Staten Island.

Christina Knight is Assistant Professor of Visual Studies and Director of the Visual Studies Program at Haverford College. She is also director of knightworks dance theater, cofounded with her sister in 2013. She is completing a book about representations of the Middle Passage in contemporary American visual art and performance.

Emily Lordi is Associate Professor of English at Vanderbilt University, a writer-at-large at *T: The New York Times Style Magazine*, and author of three books: *Black Resonance*, *Donny Hathaway Live*, and *The Meaning of Soul*.

Vuyelwa Maluleke holds a Masters in Creative Writing from the University Currently Known as Rhodes. Shortlisted for the Brunel University African Poetry Prize in 2014, she is author of the chapbook *Things We Lost in the Fire*.

Reginald McKnight won the O. Henry Award, the Drue Heinz Literature Prize, and the Whiting Writer's Award. He is the Hamilton Holmes Professor at the University of Georgia and author of *He Sleeps*, *Moustapha's Eclipse*, *I Get on the Bus*, *The Kind of Light that Shines on Texas*, and *White Boys*.

Cheswayo Mphanza's work has been featured in the *New England Review, Paris Review*, the *Hampden-Sydney Review, Lolwe, Hayden's Ferry Review*, and *Birdfeast*. A finalist for the Brunel International African Poetry Prize and a recipient of the 2017 Hurston/Wright Award for College Writers, his debut collection, *The Rinehart Frames*, won the Sillerman First Book Prize for African Poets.

Achal Prabhala is a writer based in Bangalore, India. His writing has appeared in *Chimurenga* and *Bidoun*.

Domenica Ruta is author of *With or Without You* and *Last Day*, which was named one of the 100 Best Books of 2019 by the *New York Times*. Her short fiction and essays have appeared in *Epoch*, *Ninth Letter*, and the *Indiana Review*. She teaches at Bard Early College.

Metta Sáma is author of six collections of poetry, including *Swing at your own risk* and the chapbooks *le animal and other creatures* and *After "Sleeping to Dream"/After After*. She is on the Editorial Advisory Board of Black Radish Books and is a Senior Fellow at Black Earth Institute.

Sonia Sanchez was a leading figure in the Black Arts Movement and is author of over a dozen books of poetry, as well as numerous plays. Her *Collected Poems* will be published this spring.

Izumi Suzuki (1949–1986) was a writer, actress, model, and countercultural icon in Japan. In the last decade of her life she produced an influential body of radical, punky, groundbreaking fiction.

Deborah Taffa, a citizen of the Quechan (Yuma Indian) Nation, has writing in dozens of outlets including PBS, *Salon, Huffington Post*, the *Rumpus, Brevity, A Public Space*, and the Best American series. Her memoir manuscript won the SFWP Literary Award in 2019. She teaches at Webster University and Washington University in St. Louis.

Kyoko Uchida is author of *Elsewhere*. Her poetry, prose, and translations have appeared in *Georgia Review, Prairie Schooner*, and *North American Review.*

Ocean Vuong, a MacArthur Fellow, is author of *On Earth We're Briefly Gorgeous* and *Night Sky with Exit Wounds.*

Binyavanga Wainaina (1971–2019) won the Caine Prize for African Writing and was author of *One Day I Will Write About This Place* as well as the celebrated essay "How to Write About Africa."

Yeoh Jo-Ann's first novel, *Impractical Uses of Cake*, won the Epigram Books Fiction Prize, one of Singapore's top fiction prizes, and her short stories have been included in anthologies such as *Best Singaporean Short Stories: Volume Three*. She is currently working on her second novel and a collection of short stories exploring the themes of modernity, food, and family in Southeast Asia.

Felicia Zamora is author of *I Always Carry My Bones*, winner of the 2020 Iowa Poetry Prize, *Body of Render*, winner of the Benjamin Saltman Award, and *Of Form & Gather*, winner of the Andrés Montoya Poetry Prize. She is Assistant Professor of Poetry at the University of Cincinnati and associate poetry editor for *Colorado Review.*